TCM
TURNER CLASSIC MOVIES

CHRISTMAS IN THE MOVIES

30 CLASSICS
TO CELEBRATE THE SEASON

JEREMY ARNOLD

RUNNING PRESS
PHILADELPHIA

PAGE 2: Natalie Wood and Edmund Gwenn in *Miracle on 34th Street* (1947)

OPPOSITE: James Stewart and Margaret Sullavan in *The Shop Around the Corner* (1940)

Running Press
Hachette Book Group
1290 Avenue of the Americas, New York, NY 10104
www.runningpress.com
@Running_Press

Printed in China

First Edition: October 2018

Published by Running Press, an imprint of Perseus Books, LLC, a subsidiary of Hachette Book Group, Inc. The Running Press name and logo is a trademark of the Hachette Book Group.

The Hachette Speakers Bureau provides a wide range of authors for speaking events. To find out more, go to www.hachettespeakersbureau.com or call (866) 376-6591.

The publisher is not responsible for websites (or their content) that are not owned by the publisher.

Image credits: pages 51, 74, 75 (left), 86 (bottom left), 111 (top), 112 (right), 138, 139 (bottom), 160, 163–166, 170, 171, 173–179, 180 (top), 181, 184–192, 193 (bottom left and right), 194: Courtesy Photofest; page 193 (top): Courtesy The Everett Collection; pages 33, 36 (bottom): Courtesy Ronald V. Borst/Hollywood Movie Posters; pages 14-16, 37, 56, 59-61, 90, 101-106, 115, 116, 118, 127-129, 135: Author's Collection; all other photography courtesy Turner Classic Movies, Inc.

Print book cover and interior design by Jason Kayser.

Library of Congress Control Number: 2018942424

ISBNs: 978-0-7624-9248-0 (hardcover), 978-0-7624-9249-7 (ebook)

RRD-S

10 9 8 7 6 5 4 3 2 1

CONTENTS

Publicity photo of
Robert Mitchum and Janet
Leigh promoting
Holiday Affair (1949)

INTRODUCTION

Would the holiday season feel complete without the sight of James Stewart running through the snow, shouting "Merry Christmas" to Bedford Falls? Without the longing on Peter Billingsley's face as he stares through a shop window at the air rifle of his dreams? Without Natalie Wood's skeptical yank of Kris Kringle's whiskers?

Each December, we look forward to the warm cheer that comes from reuniting with family and friends, sitting down to festive meals, exchanging presents, and revisiting our favorite holiday movies. They are as much a ritual of the season by now as candy canes and roast turkey. When we view them, we journey back to our childhoods, laugh at our quirks, and lose ourselves in tales of love and compassion. There's nostalgia in many of these stories and even in the simple act of watching them: they stir our memories of having seen them in earlier times, with earlier loved ones.

We also adore them for their buoyant endings. Knowing they end happily is not a spoiler but part of the appeal. It's what we want and expect at Christmastime—for the spirit of the season to come through and win in the end, somehow, some way. In short, these films do what the season does: bring us back and lift us up.

Motion pictures with Christmas themes date practically to the dawn of cinema. The earliest surviving example, *Santa Claus*, runs

The Christmas movie house of our memories, from *A Christmas Story* (1983)

all of seventy-six seconds and was made by British filmmaker George Albert Smith in 1898; three years later came the first known version of *A Christmas Carol*. The films have kept coming ever since, in all shapes and sizes, but the most powerful have one vital element in common: the Christmas season is not just a backdrop but plays a meaningful role in the storytelling.

The season, of course, can "mean" different things to different people, from compassion, togetherness, and nostalgia to commercialism, cynicism, and loneliness. All have been themes for great holiday movies ranging from farce to tender drama. Genre doesn't matter: musicals, westerns, fantasies, action, and horror tales can all become Christmas films with the right approach.

This book presents thirty of the best and most intriguing English-language holiday movies—beloved classics, under-the-radar gems, and a few familiar titles you may not have considered for their yuletide slants. Some were made and marketed with their holiday content in mind; many others were released with barely a mention of Christmas. A few take place entirely on the holiday; in others, it's only a short part of the running time.

For all their differences, they share some interesting patterns and similarities. Nearly half these films, for instance, were released in the 1940s. Christmas no doubt resonated on the screen in those years because it was so often used to represent romance, nostalgia, and the idea of a complete family unit—all while millions of moviegoers were separated from loved ones or rebuilding their own families.

Family, in fact, is at the center of the vast majority of films profiled in this book. In Christmas movies, families form, grow, divide, and especially reunite. They can be generally loving (*A Christmas Story*) or highly dysfunctional (*The Lion in Winter*). They can be part of an idealized past (*Meet Me in St. Louis*) or reflect a more complicated present (*The Holly and the Ivy*). They can be made up of coworkers (*The Shop Around the Corner*) or even random

strangers (*Love Actually*). Closely tied to family is the notion of the home, and as a result, many Christmas films prominently incorporate houses, sometimes to the point of the houses becoming "characters"—as in *Holiday Inn*, *Christmas in Connecticut*, and *Home Alone*. *Remember the Night* uses two houses, one inviting and one cold and dark, to make a point about the value of family. *It's a Wonderful Life* does the same, although thanks to a fantasy sequence, it's the same house in each case!

Part of the fun of these films is in seeing recognizable elements of the season arise in different ways: office holiday parties, family dinners, the exchanging of presents, and department store Santas all take on entertainingly different tones from film to film. Even the idea of the "bad Santa" appears at least as early as *Miracle on 34th Street*, in a bit part played by Percy Helton. Holiday movies are also ripe for fantasy devices, with ghosts, angels, disembodied voices, and supernatural creatures popping up in *Beyond Tomorrow*, *The Bishop's Wife*, *Gremlins*, and others. (Squirrels, for some odd reason, are played for laughs in three pictures. Who knew?)

The lonelier, more cynical aspects of the season are covered as well, sometimes with biting honesty, as in *The Apartment*—one of four titles that contain attempted or

Peter Billingsley feeling confident in *A Christmas Story* (1983)

The result is Alastair Sim dancing in his bedroom, light as a feather; James Stewart shouting "Zuzu's petals!" with glee; and Margo, in *Miracle on Main Street*, suddenly confident and determined to raise an infant.

Transformed characters seem to notice the buoyant feel in the air that comes with the season. Maybe this "glow" is what really makes Christmas movies so popular. At their most bewitching, they allow us to bask in what Celia Johnson describes in *The Holly and the Ivy* as "the first moment when you wake up" on Christmas morning, "as if during the night, while you were asleep, something had happened"—or what Danny Elfman means in *The Nightmare Before Christmas* when he sings of "that special kind of feeling in Christmasland."

As you journey through the thirty films ahead, you will find many inventive ways in which filmmakers have conjured that feeling. The journey will take you from small-town New England to the desert southwest with many stops in-between, as well as to London, Budapest, and the North Pole of our childhood imaginations. Cherished favorites await, but hopefully so do new discoveries, there to be found and added to future holiday traditions.

contemplated suicides. Even after countless viewings, *It's a Wonderful Life* tends to shock us with the trauma it inflicts upon James Stewart and many other characters. Stewart's transformation is so powerful that the joy and uplift of the ending blot out thoughts of the film's darker sections—which, of course, have helped to make the joy all the more stirring.

Transformations of characters from bitterness to compassion are perhaps the purest Christmas stories. Often they happen without anything changing in the characters' outward circumstances. Instead, it is Christmas that somehow makes them see their lives in a new context and reawaken to the point of change.

A dysfunctional family played for laughs: Chevy Chase and Mae Questel in
National Lampoon's Christmas Vacation (1989)

MIRACLE ON MAIN STREET

Columbia, 1939 • Black and White, 73 minutes

AFTER FINDING AN ABANDONED BABY ON CHRISTMAS EVE, A BURLESQUE DANCER ATTEMPTS TO TURN HER LIFE AROUND.

Director
STEVE SEKELY

Producer
JACK H. SKIRBALL

Screenplay
FREDERICK JACKSON, from an original story by SAMUEL ORNITZ and BORIS INGSTER

Starring

MARGO	Maria
WALTER ABEL	Jim
WILLIAM COLLIER SR.	Doctor
JANE DARWELL	Mrs. Herman
LYLE TALBOT	Dick
WYNNE GIBSON	Sade
VEDA ANN BORG	Flo
PAT FLAHERTY	Detective
GEORGE HUMBERT	Pepito

ABOVE: Margo takes refuge in a church on Christmas Eve. OPPOSITE: At the church on Christmas Day, Margo considers giving the baby to a woman played by Dorothy Devore, former silent star.

Christmas is a healing force in the low-budget curiosity *Miracle on Main Street*. Right off the bat, with a striking montage of yuletide festivities, the film asks the audience to view the story through the prism of the holiday. The montage ends with a religious procession in the Old Spanish Quarter of Los Angeles on Christmas Eve.

But as the procession heads into a church, the camera suddenly turns to a nearby sideshow barker, Dick, who is enticing passersby to pay ten cents for "the thrill of a lifetime"—a tacky burlesque act headlined by his wife, Maria.

That entertaining contrast sets up an oddly endearing tale. Maria and Dick soon attempt to fleece an undercover cop, causing Maria to

Margo, Walter Abel, Jane Darwell, and William Collier Sr. face off
with a welfare worker played by Ottola Nesmith.

hide in the church and pray for heavenly help; when she notices an abandoned baby lying in the manger display, she takes it with her to mask her escape. But she gradually starts to feel such attachment to the baby that she decides to keep it, drop her no-good husband, and improve her life with a respectable job. Another man will enter the picture, but what will he think if he learns of her sordid past? And how will she deal with her shady husband when he returns?

What saves *Miracle on Main Street* from being just a far-fetched melodrama (or an obvious Christ-child parable) is the film's touching way of using Christmas as an entity that pushes characters to redeem themselves. Maria finds a new will to carve out an honest life; a doctor (William Collier Sr.) grows from drunk hobo to wise philosopher; two dancers (Wynne Gibson and Veda Ann Borg) soften their cynicism; and Maria's landlady (the plucky Jane Darwell) finds a sweet maternal instinct under her crustiness. Only Dick, the villainous husband played by Lyle Talbot, is irredeemable.

Maria is played by the actress known as Margo, born in Mexico as Maria Margarita Guadalupe Teresa Estella Bolado Castilla y O'Donnell. A professional dancer from the age of nine, she helped popularize the rumba in the early 1930s by performing in nightclubs to the music of her uncle, the bandleader Xavier Cugat. By the time she made this picture, she was already well known for her screen role in *Winterset* (1936), which she had also played on Broadway, and her turn in Frank Capra's *Lost Horizon* (1937) as the woman who ages rapidly upon leaving Shangri-La. *Miracle on Main Street* is a much smaller and cheaper production than *Lost Horizon*, but Margo carries it with a committed performance as she evolves from stripper to clothing designer and mother. She even sings a lullaby.

There was some surprisingly interesting talent behind the camera as well. This was the first American film for the Hungarian director Steve Sekely, who had worked as a journalist in the 1920s before embarking on a filmmaking career through Europe, Mexico, and India. Cowriter Boris Ingster had roots stretching back to his work with the pioneering Sergei Eisenstein in their native Russia; following this movie, Ingster would direct what some consider to be the first true film noir, *Stranger on the Third Floor* (1940).

Producer Jack Skirball would decades later become a major philanthropist with a passion for interreligious and cross-cultural programs, and *Miracle on Main Street* is an early example of that interest: it was produced in two languages so as to appeal to Latin audiences. A former rabbi, Skirball transitioned to film in 1933, producing short subjects and an infamous educational documentary, *Birth of a Baby* (1938), which was banned in several states for its explicit childbirth scenes. After taking a job as head of production at the poverty-row studio Grand National Films, he formed a subsidiary, Arcadia Pictures, to produce English- and Spanish-language versions of the same scripts.

Both versions of *Miracle on Main Street* were shot at Grand National in the spring of 1939, with Margo starring in each. A few weeks later, Skirball resigned from the studio but continued to run Arcadia as an independent producer. When Grand National disbanded soon thereafter, he enticed Columbia to step in as domestic distributor.

In September 1939, Twentieth Century-Fox released the Spanish-language version, *El milagro de la calle mayor*, in South American markets. The English-language version opened in the United States a month later. Reviews were mixed: "Hokum the family will enjoy," said one. "Will please those who see it, for it has a message of happiness and hope."

Miracle on Main Street remains decidedly rough around the edges, lacking the polish of a major studio's resources, but it compensates with some unusually frank scenes for its time and an offbeat story that succeeds because its heart, like that of Maria's, is in the right place.

Holiday Moment

On Christmas morning, Maria heads back to the church to return the baby. Once there, she is so affected by the impact of the altar display, as well as by an encounter with a woman who regrets never having had a child herself, that she is overcome by a determination to keep the baby after all and turn her life around. The Maria who exits the church is newly confident and resolute. "I'm going to look out for myself, and in my own way," she declares. She is a changed woman, the film suggests, entirely because of the power of Christmas.

REMEMBER THE NIGHT

Paramount, 1940 • Black and White, 94 minutes

Director
MITCHELL LEISEN

Producer
MITCHELL LEISEN

Screenplay
PRESTON STURGES

Starring

BARBARA STANWYCK . . . . Lee Leander
FRED MacMURRAY . . . . John Sargent
BEULAH BONDI . . . . Mrs. Sargent
ELIZABETH PATTERSON . . . . Aunt Emma
STERLING HOLLOWAY . . . . Willie
WILLARD ROBERTSON . . . . . . Francis X. O'Leary
CHARLES WALDRON . . . . Judge
PAUL GUILFOYLE . . . . District Attorney

**OVER A HOLIDAY RECESS,
AN ASSISTANT DISTRICT ATTORNEY
FALLS IN LOVE WITH THE WOMAN
HE IS PROSECUTING.**

ABOVE: A happy Christmas Day with Barbara Stanwyck, Beulah Bondi, Fred MacMurray, Sterling Holloway, and Elizabeth Patterson PREVIOUS PAGE: Publicity shot of Fred MacMurray and Barbara Stanwyck

*R*emember the Night is a charmer. While it has remained for decades mysteriously under the radar, its tender romance and comedy are so skillfully blended—and its use of Christmas so poignant—that it stands among the very best holiday movies. The creative forces came together perfectly here: a witty screenplay by the great Preston Sturges; the visual touch of producer-director Mitchell Leisen, who had just made the masterful romantic comedy *Midnight* (1939); and the screen chemistry of Barbara Stanwyck and Fred MacMurray, so strong that the duo would team again for three more pictures, starting with *Double Indemnity* (1944).

Sturges's story revolves around a New York assistant district attorney (MacMurray) prosecuting a shoplifter (Stanwyck) just before the holidays. Feeling sorry that she will have to spend Christmas in jail waiting for the trial to resume, he bails her out; she has nowhere to go, so he offers to drive her to her childhood home in Indiana, as it's right on his own way. When he sees her cold and unwelcoming mother, however is, he whisks Stanwyck off for Christmas at his house. Stanwyck is bowled over by the love and affection she encounters there, and she and MacMurray start to fall in love. Hanging over both their heads is the realization that they still have to return to the city to resolve the trial. Will MacMurray purposely blow the case? Will she let him? As Sturges himself said: "Love reformed her and corrupted him."

Christmas is key to *Remember the Night*. It practically defines the inner psychologies of the two main characters. For Stanwyck, there is no such thing as Christmas at home—there's just a dead-looking house with no electricity, no smiles, a mean stepfather she's never met, and one of the iciest moms in American cinema. (She is underplayed perfectly by Georgia Caine.) For MacMurray, Christmas equates to cheer—with a boyhood house full of light, laughter, food, music, and a kind-hearted mother (the wonderful Beulah Bondi). MacMurray's Christmas feels a bit unreal, too, which is by design: it's the idealized, nostalgic

Producer-director Mitchell Leisen behind the scenes with his two stars

Christmas that Stanwyck always dreamed of and finally gets to experience.

The visual contrast between the two houses—in terms of their design and lighting—is especially striking, revealing the expertise of Leisen. A trained architect, he had worked as an art director (and costume designer) before starting his directing career, and he always kept a careful eye on set design and decor as tools to help tell his stories.

This was Leisen's second picture with a script by Sturges, after *Easy Living* (1937).

Fred MacMurray plays "Swanee River" as Barbara Stanwyck and Beulah Bondi look on.

He trimmed many scenes before shooting and deleted a few more afterward, something that always irritated Sturges and was why he resolved from then on to direct his own scripts. But Leisen was certainly intelligent enough not to make the trims haphazardly. Biographer David Chierichetti has written that Leisen reshaped the script to the personas and abilities of his two stars, which had the effect of making MacMurray less heroic and Stanwyck a bit more dominant than Sturges had envisioned.

Leisen wrapped production eight days ahead of schedule and $50,000 under budget. He attributed this not to the script pruning but to Barbara Stanwyck's professionalism. "[She]

Barbara Stanwyck and Fred MacMurray welcome a friend.

TOP: A pivotal moment for Fred MacMurray and Barbara Stanwyck as bit player Kate Drain Lawson looks on

BOTTOM: Fred MacMurray tries to sweet-talk judge Charles Waldron while Barbara Stanwyck fires up a distraction.

was the greatest," he said. "She never blew one line through the whole picture. . . . We never once had to wait for her to finish with the hairdresser or the makeup man. . . . She set that kind of pace and everybody worked harder, trying to outdo her."

Sturges often visited the set and got to know Stanwyck well. She later recounted that he was already planning to work with her again: "One day he said to me, 'Someday I'm going to write a real screwball comedy for you.' *Remember the Night* was a delightful comedy, swell for me and Fred MacMurray, but hardly a screwball, and I replied that nobody would ever think of writing anything like that for me—a murderess, sure. But he said, 'You just wait.'" A year later, Sturges was directing Stanwyck in *The Lady Eve* (1941), one of the best movies either of them ever made.

Perhaps the only blemish on *Remember the Night* is its inclusion of a character named Rufus, MacMurray's valet, who is presented as a black stereotype. Billed as "Snowflake," his stage name, he is played by actor Fred Toones, a familiar face to audiences for two decades. He appeared with and without credit in more than two hundred films, many of them at Republic, where he was under contract for several years.

Remember the Night opened in early January 1940, the same time of year that the story within the movie winds down. The *New York Times* called it "the real curtain-raiser for 1940," and the film was a hit. Preston Sturges quipped that he knew exactly why: "It had quite a lot of schmaltz, a good dose of schmerz, and just enough schmutz to make it box office."

Holiday Moment

Of the handful of songs in this movie, the most heartwarming is "The End of a Perfect Day." After dinner on a snowy Christmas Eve, in the living room by the tree, Stanwyck starts to play the piano. Sterling Holloway sings, the others join in, and all is right with the world.

THE SHOP AROUND THE CORNER

MGM, 1940 • Black and White, 99 minutes

S1121-2

BICKERING COWORKERS AT A BUDAPEST STORE DON'T REALIZE THEY ARE FALLING FOR EACH OTHER AS ANONYMOUS PEN PALS.

Director
ERNST LUBITSCH

Producer
ERNST LUBITSCH

Screenplay
SAMSON RAPHAELSON, based on a play by NIKOLAUS LASZLO

Starring

MARGARET SULLAVAN	Klara Novak
JAMES STEWART	Alfred Kralik
FRANK MORGAN	Hugo Matuschek
JOSEPH SCHILDKRAUT	Ferencz Vadas
SARA HADEN	Flora
FELIX BRESSART	Pirovitch
WILLIAM TRACY	Pepi Katona
INEZ COURTNEY	Ilona

One of the great romantic comedies, *The Shop Around the Corner* is also a sparkling holiday film. It's set in the weeks leading up to Christmas, which becomes a steadily increasing visual presence—just as the central relationship between Klara (Margaret Sullavan) and Alfred (James Stewart) intensifies, too. When the yuletide imagery eventually fills the screen, for the story's final act set on Christmas Eve, their relationship reaches a tipping point. The irony is that for this couple, an "intensifying" relationship means growing irritation. As coworkers at a Budapest dry-goods store, they have been quarreling with each other nonstop—about everything. What they don't know is that as anonymous pen pals, they have meanwhile been falling deeply in love.

Beneath the humor of that setup is a poignant reality—that these bickering characters are actually sensitive souls yearning for connection. At a certain point, Alfred figures out that Klara is his secret lover, and he is profoundly moved by the realization. He now sees her, and himself, in a new light. He tries to express this with the tender line, "People seldom go to the trouble of scratching the surface of things to find the inner truth." But Klara, still in the dark about the situation, brings the moment back to comedy: "Well, I really wouldn't care to scratch your surface, Mr. Kralik."

ABOVE: Some of the Matuschek and Company "family": Inez Courtney, James Stewart, William Tracy, Sara Haden, and Felix Bressart. OPPOSITE: The chemistry of Margaret Sullavan and James Stewart was "red-hot," according to Louis B. Mayer.

If any filmmaker could navigate such complicated layers of subtext in a story, a scene, or a single dialogue exchange, it was Ernst Lubitsch, Hollywood's reigning master of sophisticated comedy. He considered *The Shop Around the Corner* his proudest accomplishment, later writing, "Never did I make a picture in which the atmosphere and the characters were truer." His interest went beyond just the Klara-Alfred romance; the film is also the story of the entire group of employees at Matuschek and Company, from Mr. Matuschek on down to Pepi

Frank Morgan as Mr. Matuschek amid the snowy Christmas rush

MGM to make *Ninotchka* (1939), but with the provision that the deal also include *Parfumerie*, which his frequent writing collaborator Samson Raphaelson turned into a screenplay.

Lubitsch always wanted Stewart and Sullavan for his leads. In their two previous pictures together, they had displayed that most precious of screen commodities: chemistry. As Louis B. Mayer said upon viewing their second film, *The Shopworn Angel* (1938), "Why, they're red-hot when they get in front of a camera. I don't know what the hell it is, but it sure jumps off the screen." Lubitsch admired how generous they were as actors, never trying to upstage each other. The stars were old friends from their East Coast theater days. Sullavan had gone to Hollywood first and quickly become a star; when Stewart arrived, she helped him refine his acting for the camera and even demanded that Universal cast him in their first pairing, *Next Time We Love* (1936). By *The Shop Around the Corner*, Stewart was a major star himself. He always had a real-life crush on Sullavan, once saying that he would never marry until he found a girl like her. (He did marry, in 1949.)

The rest of the cast is filled with superb supporting players such as Felix Bressart, as Stewart's fellow employee and best friend, and

the errand boy. They all have their workplace crises and interpersonal dramas, but deep down they are like a family, a sentiment that comes to dominate. This subject matter was deeply personal for Lubitsch, who made the film as a way to pay tribute to his own father's long-ago shop in Berlin, where Lubitsch had worked as a boy.

The picture originated as a Hungarian play, *Parfumerie.* Lubitsch personally bought the rights in 1938, intending to make it as an independent production. After having trouble finding a studio to collaborate, he signed with

Margaret Sullavan and James Stewart start out hating each other.

Joseph Schildkraut as a pompous clerk. Pervasive bit player Charles Halton turns up as an investigator—he would later appear in *It's a Wonderful Life* (1946) as the bank examiner—but the scene stealer here is Frank Morgan, in perhaps his finest hour. Best known as the wizard in *The Wizard of Oz* (1939), Morgan was an omnipresent character actor stretching from the silent era to his death in 1949, with a constant churn of secondary roles in major films and leading roles in smaller ones. As Mr. Matuschek, he shades his usual comic bumbler with tenderness and heartbreak as he learns that his wife is having an affair.

Because most of the film is set in the shop, Lubitsch was able to shoot in sequence, helping the actors build their performances even more fluidly. The movie premiered at Radio City Music Hall and became a major hit. In later years it was remade as *In the Good Old Summertime* (1949), a musical with Judy Garland and Van Johnson, and *You've Got Mail* (1998), starring Meg Ryan and Tom Hanks, but the original has endured best. No doubt this is due to the unique wit and sensitivity of Ernst Lubitsch, especially his talent for finding the compassion lurking beneath the most guarded human surfaces.

TCM's Robert Osborne often cited *The Shop Around the Corner* as his own favorite holiday movie. "It automatically puts me in a jolly yuletime mood," he once said. "But it doesn't have to be Christmas to really love this film."

Christmas decor pops up more frequently as the story—and the Stewart/Sullavan relationship—intensifies.

Holiday Moment

When Mr. Matuschek realizes that both he and Rudy, the new errand boy, have no place to go on Christmas Eve, he invites him to an impromptu dinner. Frank Morgan's enthusiasm is heartwarming, and his fervent recitation of the dinner menu alone is sure to leave anyone hungry.

BEYOND TOMORROW

RKO, 1940 • Black and White, 84 minutes

**THREE OLD MEN HELP GUIDE
A YOUNG COUPLE THROUGH A
RELATIONSHIP—EVEN FROM BEYOND
THE GRAVE.**

Director

A. EDWARD SUTHERLAND

Producer

LEE GARMES

Screenplay

ADELE COMANDINI, based on an original story
by MILDRED CRAM and ADELE COMANDINI

Starring

CHARLES WINNINGER	Michael O'Brien
RICHARD CARLSON	James Houston
MARIA OUSPENSKAYA	Madam Tanya
JEAN PARKER	Jean Lawrence
HELEN VINSON	Arlene Terry
C. AUBREY SMITH	Allan Chadwick
HARRY CAREY	George Melton
ROD LA ROCQUE	Phil Hubert
WILLIAM BAKEWELL	David Chadwick

Christmas dominates the first portion of *Beyond Tomorrow*, driving the warmth, romance, and tenderness that build on screen. It's Christmas Eve in New York City, and three wealthy old men—business partners and friends—face a lonely dinner when their guests cancel at the last moment. As they lament the waning number of friends they have at all anymore, the most sentimental of the three (Charles Winninger) hatches an idea: each will toss a wallet containing ten dollars and a business card to the snowy sidewalk below. "Maybe they'll bring back somebody to have dinner with us," he exclaims. "What, strangers out of the street?" asks C. Aubrey Smith. "There are no strangers on Christmas Eve," replies Winninger. "Nobody'll come back with them," predicts Harry Carey, the most Scrooge-like of the bunch.

Carey is wrong, of course, for two wallets are indeed brought back by two honest souls: first by Richard Carlson, playing a rodeo performer trying to save enough money to move back to Texas, and then by Jean Parker, as a children's clinic worker. Because this is a heartwarming

C. Aubrey Smith, Harry Carey, and Charles Winninger toss their wallets on Christmas Eve.

little fable of a movie, these two just so happen to be young, attractive, and alone in the city, and it's clear that love will blossom. They stay for dinner, sip Tom and Jerry cocktails by the fire, and sing Christmas songs, even inviting some roving musicians inside. On Christmas morning, the joyousness continues as the group spends hours playing with the orphans at the children's clinic.

Months swirl by, and the film takes an intriguing shift. Struck by tragedy, the three men spend the rest of the story as ghosts, watch-

ing in dismay as things go wrong for the young lovers: Carlson is falling in with the wrong crowd and losing sight of his love with Parker while he launches a singing career. As the spirits start to learn what comes next for themselves, Winninger feels compelled to perhaps stay behind and guide the couple back together, even if it means relinquishing his own peaceful afterlife. More twists follow, but suffice it to say that the depth of feeling from the opening sequence—fostered by Christmastime—is what

Bad girl Helen Vinson tempts Richard Carlson.

the characters, the film, and the audience all want to regain.

Critics in 1940 did not receive *Beyond Tomorrow* very well, finding the shift to fantasy too outlandish. In truth, the story is presented enough like a fable from the very beginning that the appearance of ghosts—a common Christmas movie trope—seems more captivating than jarring. It also helps that the spirit world is presented with great charm and technical virtuosity.

The whimsical screenplay was written by Mildred Cram, a romance novelist who had just scored an Oscar nomination for *Love Affair* (1939), and Adele Comandini, who would later write *Christmas in Connecticut* (1945), but the key creative force here was really the producer, Lee Garmes. Known chiefly as an innovative cinematographer of lush films like *Shanghai Express* (1932), his handful of producing (and occasionally directing) credits are all offbeat, visually arresting works; *Beyond Tomorrow* is no exception. Stephen Goosson's art direction is beautifully appointed and imaginative, especially for such a low-budget film, and the photography by Lester White, who no doubt worked closely with Garmes, is excellent.

The transparent "ghost" effects were much praised at the time. *Variety* declared that "industry insiders will be intrigued by the

Maria Ouspenskaya, Jean Parker, and Richard Carlson, saddened by the men's deaths

technical achievement," and a 1940 *American Cinematographer* article revealed that the effects were created not by double exposures but by filming reflections of actors in mirror-image sets through angled glass—an age-old magic technique known as "Pepper's Ghost." It's especially effective in the shots that combine the ghosts with real people.

Though it lacks major stars, *Beyond Tomorrow* boasts a great group of character actors, many with careers stretching deep into the silent era. Harry Carey had not only been a

RIGHT: Lobby card depicting the three ghosts

BELOW: The three men and their young new friends on Christmas Eve

silent star but had just been Oscar-nominated for his role as the vice president in *Mr. Smith Goes to Washington* (1939). Maria Ouspenskaya, who delivers a typically intense turn as the only character who can perceive the ghosts, had also just been nominated, for *Love Affair.*

Twenty-seven-year-old Richard Carlson was still over a decade away from the stardom that would come with science-fiction classics and a hit TV series, but he is an endearing presence and sings several songs very well (he was not dubbed), including "Jeanie with the Light Brown Hair" and "It's Raining Dreams."

Beyond Tomorrow, an independent production distributed by RKO, was not marketed with its Christmas theme. It opened in May 1940 and expanded across the country into the autumn, before becoming more or less forgotten. Much

Jean Parker with orphans on Christmas Day

later it fell into the public domain and found a new life on television and home video, at one point sporting a new title, *Beyond Christmas*, which was never intended by any of its creators.

Holiday Moment

"Jingle Bells" has probably never been sung onscreen with as much gusto—or in as many simultaneous languages—as it is here. Carlson suggests the song during a Christmas Eve singalong and everybody joins in, including Maria Ouspenskaya and the rest of the household staff, who are Russian, German, and Italian. The result emanates such joy that even grumpy Harry Carey, sitting by the window with his back to the others, can't resist singing a few bars.

THE MAN WHO CAME TO DINNER

Warner Bros., 1942 • Black and White, 112 minutes

A WITTY BUT INSUFFERABLE AUTHOR INJURES HIS LEG AND IS CONFINED TO THE HOUSE OF AN OHIO COUPLE OVER THE CHRISTMAS HOLIDAY.

Director
WILLIAM KEIGHLEY

Executive Producer
HAL B. WALLIS

Screenplay
JULIUS J. and PHILIP G. EPSTEIN, from the stage play by GEORGE S. KAUFMAN and MOSS HART

Starring

BETTE DAVIS.................Maggie Cutler

ANN SHERIDAN............Lorraine Sheldon

MONTY WOOLLEY........Sheridan Whiteside

RICHARD TRAVIS.............Bert Jefferson

JIMMY DURANTE.....................Banjo

BILLIE BURKE...........Mrs. Ernest Stanley

REGINALD GARDINER.........Beverly Carlton

ELISABETH FRASER.............June Stanley

GRANT MITCHELL........Mr. Ernest Stanley

GEORGE BARBIER...............Dr. Bradley

MARY WICKES.................Miss Preen

Verbal zingers fly off the screen in *The Man Who Came to Dinner*, a movie brimming with humor and wit—from sophisticated takedowns and satirical jabs at real-life personalities to the sudden screen entrance of an octopus. In fact, anything imaginable could enter the frame and the film would find a way of justifying it.

The comedy centers on Sheridan Whiteside, a respected author and radio commentator known as the "first man of American letters." He's also arrogant, rude, and demanding. When he arrives in the town of Mesalia, Ohio, shortly before Christmas to deliver a lecture, he reluctantly heads to dinner at the house of "Midwestern

Monty Woolley and Bette Davis square off: "You know, Sherry, you have one great advantage over everyone else in the world: You've never had to meet Sheridan Whiteside."

barbarians" Mr. and Mrs. Stanley, only to slip on the ice and injure his leg. As a result, he's confined to a wheelchair for ten days in the Stanley home—or "moldy mortuary," as he calls it. He wreaks havoc by taking over the household and its staff, installing his private secretary, and inviting over one eccentric friend after another. (The Stanleys, he declares, can use the back staircase.) Sheridan is so insufferable that only his secretary, Maggie Cutler, can put up with him.

When she falls for a local newspaper editor and talks about leaving her job, he hatches a scheme to stop her—and she counters with a plan of her own.

This farce was adapted from a massive Broadway hit by George S. Kaufman and Moss Hart, the team responsible for *You Can't Take It with You*. The writers based Sheridan Whiteside squarely on their friend Alexander Woollcott, the acerbic literary and drama critic, who had spent a weekend at Hart's Pennsylvania estate issuing outrageous demands and complaints. They drew from other celebrity friends, too: the diva-like actress Lorraine Sheldon was based on stage star Gertrude Lawrence; a writer character, Beverly Carlton, was modeled on Noël Coward; and a wisecracking, skirt-chasing entertainer named Banjo was based on Harpo Marx.

Before the play even finished its 739 performances, Warner Bros. bought the screen rights for a record $250,000 and assigned the brothers Julius and Philip Epstein to craft a script. (They would soon afterward start writing *Casablanca* [1942].) Casting became a headache. The play had starred Monty Woolley, a known Broadway personality, but he had only played small roles in movies, and executive producer Hal Wallis wanted a recognizable movie star. He

Mary Wickes made a stellar film debut as Miss Preen,
the nurse, after playing her for two years on Broadway.

went about testing Charles Laughton, Laird Cregar, Fredric March, and John Barrymore, but none seemed right. (Barrymore was in such poor health he needed cue cards to speak his lines.) Orson Welles, then in postproduction on *Citizen Kane* (1941), strongly desired the role and even wanted to direct, but RKO refused to loan him out. After two months of getting nowhere, Wallis decided to go with Monty Woolley after all.

To protect this gamble, he flanked Woolley with two major female stars: Bette Davis, who had yearned to play Maggie Cutler opposite John Barrymore, and Ann Sheridan. This was a rare comedy and ensemble role for Davis, especially at this point of her career, when she was starring in highly dramatic parts. It was a change of pace for Sheridan as well, who steals her scenes as Lorraine Sheldon by playing hilariously over the top. At one point, Jimmy Durante as Banjo refers to her as the "Oomph Girl"—Warner Bros.' real nickname for Sheridan.

Two other actresses were imported from Broadway with Woolley: Mary Wickes, making her screen debut in a career-defining role as the nurse, Miss Preen, and Ruth Vivian as Harriet Stanley, a sweet little lady with a pitch-dark secret. Mostly, though, this is Woolley's show, and he tears into his role with gusto.

The Man Who Came to Dinner is great fun to watch at Christmastime—for the seasonal backdrop; for the laughs in seeing Sheridan Whiteside receive Christmas presents from the likes of Winston Churchill, Deanna Durbin, and Somerset Maugham; and for its biting humor. With so many sentimental movie takes on Christmas, especially in the 1940s, the dose of irreverence is refreshing.

Grant Mitchell (center) and Billie Burke (right) interrupt Monty Woolley as he prepares his radio broadcast.

Holiday Moment

On Christmas Eve, Sheridan prepares to deliver a radio broadcast from the Stanley living room. With thirty seconds to go, Maggie runs out in romantic despair, Mr. Stanley charges downstairs to yell at Sheridan for butting into his kids' lives, the local doctor walks in to inquire if now's a good time to start discussing his book of memoirs, four penguins waddle in from the next room, and a nine-boy choir rushes into place to start singing "Silent Night." Sheridan calmly begins: "On this eve of eves, when my own heart is overflowing with peace and kindness, I think it is most fitting to tell once again the story of that still and lustrous night."

This is something of a mini version of the famous Marx Brothers stateroom scene in *A Night at the Opera* (1935), which had also been cowritten by George S. Kaufman. Once again he crams an absurd number of people into a room, but he also uses the serene image of Christmas to create perfect comedy contrast.

HOLIDAY INN

Paramount, 1942 • Black and White, 100 minutes

A SINGER OPENS A CONNECTICUT NIGHTSPOT THAT OPERATES JUST ON HOLIDAYS, THEN MUST DEAL WITH HIS OLD MUSICAL PARTNER TRYING TO STEAL HIS GIRLFRIEND.

Director
MARK SANDRICH

Producer
MARK SANDRICH

Screenplay
CLAUDE BINYON and ELMER RICE, based on an idea by IRVING BERLIN

Starring
BING CROSBY . . . . Jim Hardy
FRED ASTAIRE. . . . . Ted Hanover
MARJORIE REYNOLDS . . . . Linda Mason
VIRGINIA DALE . . . . Lila Dixon
WALTER ABEL . . . . Danny Reed
LOUISE BEAVERS. . . . . Mamie

The two stars with Walter Abel (right) as their comically jittery manager. Abel was a versatile actor: he had played a dramatic role in the 1939 Christmas film *Miracle on Main Street*.

Holiday Inn is expert entertainment from what its director called the "ABC of American musical comedy": Fred Astaire, Irving Berlin, and Bing Crosby. It brims with song, dance, humor, and cheery yuletide scenes—and boasts the screen debut of the most popular Christmas song of all time.

Christmas makes three appearances in a story that spans two years and one week, but the movie also pays tribute to seven other American holidays, with musical numbers to represent them

all. Astaire and Crosby play a song-and-dance team who are also romantic rivals; after Crosby leaves the act and moves to Connecticut, where he opens a rustic nightclub that operates only on holidays, Astaire shows up and they fall into a rivalry over Crosby's new dance partner, played by Marjorie Reynolds.

The film was Irving Berlin's idea. He first conceived it as a follow-up to *As Thousands Cheer*, a hit Broadway revue that he and Moss Hart had written in 1933, but it wasn't until he

TOP: Bing Crosby sings "Be Careful, It's My Heart," while Fred Astaire dances behind his back with Marjorie Reynolds.

BOTTOM: Fred's got eyes for Marjorie, and Bing isn't happy about it.

pitched it to Paramount director Mark Sandrich as a vehicle for Crosby that the idea gained any traction. Sandrich loved it and immediately thought of Astaire for the other male lead. Sandrich had directed him in five Astaire-Rogers musicals at RKO, and they had a strong rapport. Paramount balked at the cost of using two superstars in one film but Sandrich persisted, ultimately agreeing to make up for the cost by casting two inexpensive, barely known actresses as the female leads: Marjorie Reynolds, who had been making B westerns, and Virginia Dale, who had played only a few minor film roles. The ladies acquitted themselves well, injecting their own energy and sass into a lively picture.

Sandrich's expertise shows in the smooth transitions in and out of musical numbers and in the many jumps to different time periods of the story. The consistent greatness of the music helps in this regard, too. Berlin supplied twelve new songs plus two old ones ("Lazy" and "Easter Parade"), making *Holiday Inn* practically wall-to-wall musical numbers. He even wrote the music played by the band in the background of the nightclub, which was led by Bing's brother Bob Crosby.

One of the joys of the movie is the chemistry between Crosby and Astaire. True to their screen images, Bing is the easygoing, ever-lazy, romantic singer, while Fred is the more cocky and aggressive

Fred Astaire in his spectacular dance "Let's Say It with Firecrackers"

romantic dancer, and they duel entertainingly for the same girl by using those respective strengths. In their opening number, "I'll Capture Your Heart Singing," they take turns singing and dancing for Virginia Dale. For the Valentine's Day song, "Be Careful, It's My Heart," Bing sings at the piano to Marjorie Reynolds, unaware that Fred is dancing with her behind his back.

Irving Berlin was sure that "Be Careful, It's My Heart" would be the breakout hit of the soundtrack. It did well, but the sensation was ultimately "White Christmas." Its melancholy

Bing Crosby, Marjorie Reynolds, Fred Astaire, and Virginia Dale wish you a happy new year.

Holiday Inn has plenty of other memorable numbers, including Astaire's reprise of "You're Easy to Dance With." Astaire later wrote that since his character was supposed to be inebriated, he drank two shots of bourbon before the first take and one more before each succeeding take; they filmed seven takes and used the last one. For the Independence Day number "Let's Say It with Firecrackers," Astaire danced while setting off firecrackers on the floor all around him. To perfect the timing, he rehearsed for three days and performed thirty-eight takes.

One number that has not endured is "Abraham," the Lincoln's Birthday song performed in blackface by Astaire and Reynolds. At the time, this was seen as a link to the minstrel tradition in popular music that had influenced Irving Berlin. But times did gradually change, and it's telling that by 1954, when this film was loosely updated as *White Christmas*, "Abraham" was performed without blackface as a modern dance by Vera-Ellen and John Brascia.

Crosby and Astaire would reunite for *Blue Skies* in 1946, again with an Irving Berlin soundtrack that included "White Christmas," but *Holiday Inn* is the more special film, with a stronger story, faster pace, and holiday charm to spare.

tone may have been influenced by the death of Berlin's infant son on Christmas Day in 1928, but it was originally written to be more humorous—with a verse about missing East Coast Christmases while stuck in sun-drenched Beverly Hills. The song was first heard publicly on December 25, 1941, when Crosby performed it on the radio. In May 1942, he made a commercial recording that was released just before the film opened that summer. By the end of the year, it was the top song in the country and a constant presence on Armed Forces Radio, reaching soldiers across the world. A few months later, it won the Academy Award for Best Song.

A romantic Christmas moment: "White Christmas," with Bing Crosby and Marjorie Reynolds

Holiday Moment

If there had been any inkling that "White Christmas" would be the movie's most enduring song, perhaps it would have been presented on a bigger scale. Instead, it's performed intimately, used to link two characters in love in a yuletide setting. Crosby sits at a piano, in front of a roaring fire, in a cozy inn, with a Christmas tree in front of him and Marjorie Reynolds beside him. He sings to her, and then they sing together (with Reynolds dubbed by Martha Mears) in lush harmony.

MEET ME IN ST. LOUIS

MGM, 1944 • Color, 113 minutes

A FAMILY IN 1903 ST. LOUIS
FACES THE POSSIBILITY OF A MOVE
TO NEW YORK.

Director

VINCENTE MINNELLI

Producer

ARTHUR FREED

Screenplay

IRVING BRECHER and FRED F. FINKLEHOFFE,
based on the book by SALLY BENSON

Starring

JUDY GARLAND	Esther Smith
MARGARET O'BRIEN	"Tootie" Smith
MARY ASTOR	Mrs. Anna Smith
LUCILLE BREMER	Rose Smith
LEON AMES	Mr. Alonzo Smith
TOM DRAKE	John Truett
MARJORIE MAIN	Katie
HARRY DAVENPORT	Grandpa
JUNE LOCKHART	Lucille Ballard
HENRY H. DANIELS JR.	Lon Smith Jr.
JOAN CARROLL	Agnes Smith

Judy Garland comforts a distraught Margaret O'Brien amid her snowpeople.

The two and a half minutes of screen time in which Judy Garland sings "Have Yourself a Merry Little Christmas" would be enough to catapult *Meet Me in St. Louis* to the front ranks of holiday classics. As it happens, the film devotes twenty-five minutes to the season, all of them set on Christmas Eve and all rich with meaning in a story built entirely around themes of family and nostalgia.

In fact, the story essentially *is* "family." There's no real plot to speak of, just a series of episodes that play out in the lives of the Smith family in 1903 St. Louis: a mother and father, a son and four daughters, a grandfather, and the family cook. Will the boy next door notice the girl who pines for him? Will her sister get a marriage proposal? Will the youngest girl work up the courage on Halloween to approach the front door of a scary neighbor (and his "fierce bulldog")? The film makes incidents like these feel like major events—because they are, to the young characters experiencing them. Through it all, their family comes to feel like a refuge. The closest

TOP: Mary Astor and Leon Ames sing "You and I," written by Arthur Freed and Nacio Herb Brown. Freed dubbed Ames's singing voice in this scene.

BOTTOM: Behind the scenes of a family dinner sequence

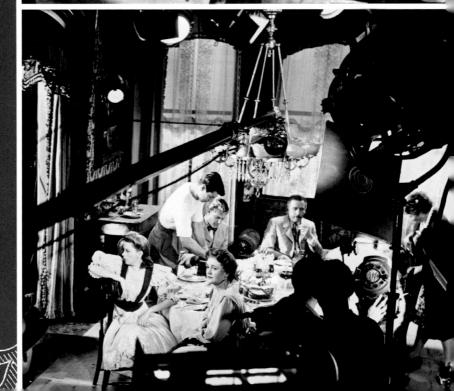

thing to a larger plot—the possibility of the Smiths uprooting to New York—isn't even introduced until well into the second hour, and it takes a crisis on Christmas, that ultimate family day, to resolve it.

The emphasis on family, especially from the perspective of the children, comes straight from the movie's source material, a series of *New Yorker* articles by Sally Benson based on her childhood that she compiled into a book. Producer Arthur Freed bought the rights and set George Cukor to direct, but when Cukor was drafted into the war effort, the job fell to Vincente Minnelli. This was Minnelli's third feature, and he succeeded in integrating the musical numbers into the story so seamlessly that for these characters, singing is as natural as walking or breathing. The result was one of the most influential musicals of its day.

Judy Garland, then twenty-two, famously resisted taking on the role of seventeen-year-old Esther Smith because she had no wish to play another teenager. But MGM chief Louis B. Mayer stepped in to persuade her, and Garland was ultimately glad: it wound up being her favorite role, and she fell in love with Minnelli and married him the next year. She also got to sing "Have Yourself a Merry Little Christmas," a rendition that is among the most indelible

The Smith living room dressed for the Christmas sequence

of all Christmas screen moments not just for its beautiful melody and Garland's emotional performance, but for the words that she sings. Garland herself played a role in shaping the lyrics, which originally were quite a bit darker.

Hugh Martin had written the song after his songwriting partner, Ralph Blane, encouraged him not to give up when Martin couldn't figure out how to resolve the melody. Martin reread the script and thought about the sadness of that moment—Esther trying to comfort Tootie (Margaret O'Brien), who is dejected about leaving St. Louis and wonders if Santa Claus will know how to find them in New York. (The

Publicity shot of Margaret O'Brien reading sheet music

character of Tootie was based on Sally Benson herself.) The rest of the song, and the words, now came to Martin, and everyone agreed the result was beautiful but also *too* sad. Garland said, "If I sing that lyric to little Margaret O'Brien, the audience will think I'm a monster." She asked Blane to change it, but he resisted. After a week or two, the impasse was ended when costar Tom Drake sat Martin down and told him to stop being "a stubborn idiot."

The irony is that the final version still comes off as strikingly bittersweet. Its melancholic feel, conjuring loss and sorrow beneath the nostalgia,

injects a dose of honesty into the film's image of Christmas—not to mention childhood. Further, the song is still sad enough to prompt Tootie to run outside and whack the heads off her "snowpeople," an image of genuine trauma. Margaret O'Brien, all of seven years old, delivers an astoundingly professional performance, and she was given a special Academy Award for it.

The picture was nominated for four other Oscars, including Best Screenplay, Color Cinematography, Score, and Song—and another irony is that the song was not "Have Yourself a Merry Little Christmas" but "The Trolley Song," which was the immediate breakout hit. "The Boy Next Door" was also extremely popular, but it would take several more years until "Have Yourself a Merry Little Christmas" became a true standard. It has since been recorded by countless other artists, usually with a set of still more upbeat lyrics that Martin wrote in 1957.

Ultimately, *Meet Me in St. Louis* keeps true to its notion of the importance of family. Judy Garland later said that the winter sequence reminded her of her own childhood in snowy Minnesota, where she grew up with two sisters. "To those of us with wonderful family memories," she said, "the picture was a nice reminder. To others it showed what family life can be at its best. To me, it was both."

Holiday Moment

"Have Yourself a Merry Little Christmas" remains a beloved song of the holiday season. Here are the lyrics as Judy Garland sang them, followed by the original, darker, unused version.

As performed by Judy Garland:

Have yourself a merry little Christmas

Let your heart be light

Next year all our troubles will be out of sight

Have yourself a merry little Christmas

Make the yuletide gay

Next year all our troubles will be miles away

Once again as in olden days

Happy golden days of yore

Faithful friends who were dear to us

Will be near to us once more

Someday soon we all will be together

If the fates allow

Until then, we'll have to muddle through somehow

So have yourself a merry little Christmas now

Original version:

Have yourself a merry little Christmas

It may be your last

Next year we may all be living in the past

Have yourself a merry little Christmas

Pop that champagne cork

Next year we may all be living in New York

No good times like the olden days

Happy golden days of yore

Faithful friends who were dear to us

Will be near to us no more

But at least we all will be together

If the Lord allows

From now on, we'll have to muddle through somehow

So have yourself a merry little Christmas now

I'LL BE SEEING YOU

United Artists, 1944 • Black and White, 85 minutes

**A MAN AND A WOMAN, EACH
MENTALLY FRAGILE,
MEET ON A TRAIN JUST
BEFORE CHRISTMAS AND START
A TENUOUS ROMANCE.**

Director
WILLIAM DIETERLE

Producer
DORE SCHARY

Screenplay
MARION PARSONNET, based on a radio
play by CHARLES MARTIN

Starring

GINGER ROGERS ....Mary Marshall
JOSEPH COTTEN .... Zachary Morgan
SHIRLEY TEMPLE........... Barbara Marshall
SPRING BYINGTON .... Mrs. Marshall
TOM TULLY .... Mr. Marshall
DARE HARRIS .... Lieutenant Bruce
CHILL WILLS ....Swanson
KENNY BOWERS ....Sailor

I'll Be Seeing You was a major commercial and critical hit during the 1944 holiday season, grossing well over $3 million, but the cameras might never have rolled on this touching romance had it not been for the determination of Dore Schary. The producer had recently left MGM to head a new production unit for David O. Selznick called Vanguard Films, meant as a home for somewhat lower-budget movies. Selznick promised creative freedom: he would leave Schary alone until the rough-cut stage.

For his first project, Schary purchased a radio play called Double Furlough, which blended a romantic plot with topical social issues. In the story, a man and a woman meet on a train just before the holidays. He's a combat veteran on furlough from a hospital, where he's being treated for what would now be called post-traumatic stress disorder, which has caused him severe mental

BELOW: Shirley Temple and Spring Byington, as daughter and mother, in a worried moment
OPPOSITE: Joseph Cotten and Ginger Rogers dance on New Year's Eve.

anguish. She is on a ten-day leave from prison, where she's been serving a six-year term for manslaughter—the result of having defended herself from certain sexual assault by her employer. They wind up traveling to the same town and slowly falling in love over the Christmas period, but they hide the full truth about themselves for fear of driving the other away.

James Cagney and Gertrude Lawrence had played these roles on the radio in October 1943, and Schary felt that Selznick contract star Joseph Cotten would be perfect for the film. Selznick, however, was skeptical about the entire concept and started sending over endless pages of notes and changes, adding that he didn't want to attach Cotten to what he considered a subpar script that wouldn't attract any other major talent. Schary threatened to resign, and Selznick relented. Within weeks, Schary had secured an A-list star, Joan Fontaine, and an A-list director, John Cromwell, which convinced Selznick to allow the use of Cotten after all. Fontaine and Cromwell were eventually replaced by Ginger Rogers and William Dieterle, keeping the film at its suddenly sky-high cost, and Selznick now agreed to cast another of his contract stars, Shirley Temple, for the role of Rogers's niece. Despite the confrontations, Schary considered Selznick "the smartest and most gifted" producer in Hollywood, "a master of film editing [who] had exquisite taste . . . and a willingness to dare."

During production, Schary and Dieterle experienced some friction, too, especially when the director started shooting hallucination scenes that were not in the script. Schary ordered him to stop. Dieterle complained straight to Selznick, who listened to both men, then ordered Dieterle to do it Schary's way or quit. Selznick's instincts were correct on this one. In the finished film, Cotten's hallucinations are expressed by vivid sound effects and his inner thoughts are heard in voiceover (which Cotten delivers expertly, no doubt due to his experience as a radio actor for Orson Welles in the 1930s). The result is more powerful because it makes the audience *imagine* the trauma.

Christmas plays a subtle but significant role in *I'll Be Seeing You*, with the backdrop of the holidays fostering a general atmosphere of goodwill, patience, and understanding among the characters. Cotten and Rogers play damaged souls trying to heal and carefully navigate the vulnerabilities of love, and there's a gentleness about their interactions that feels linked to the season. Rogers's aunt and uncle, beautifully played by Spring Byington and Tom Tully, seem

TOP LEFT: Ginger Rogers with Spring Byington, as her aunt **BOTTOM LEFT:** Ginger Rogers welcomed by Tom Tully, as her uncle **RIGHT:** The studio touted Shirley Temple in "her first grown-up part," as seen in this rare publicity shot in which her "little-girl" image is put to rest in a painting.

Ginger Rogers feels a little troubled despite the Christmas tree.

close-up, with a blonde-wigged extra filling in for Rogers in the foreground. Temple later wrote that Cukor filmed twelve takes, chastising and insulting her all the while. Finally he stopped, put an arm around her, and admitted he had simply been using a technique to build up the hysterical effect he required. Temple was not happy, but the scene, and her performance overall, drew very strong notices. She turned sixteen during production, and the film was touted as "her first grown-up part." It even includes several lines of dialogue poking fun at her for not being so little anymore. ("I never would have known you!" Rogers exclaims upon seeing her.)

At first the picture was to be called *I'll See You Again*, from the 1929 standard by Noël Coward, but Coward asked for too much money for the use of the song. Selznick and Schary then thought of the 1938 Sammy Fain-Irving Kahal song "I'll Be Seeing You," which had just become a number-one hit, thanks to a new recording by Bing Crosby. The song and the title no doubt helped lure people to theaters, but it's not hard to see why the movie itself touched wartime audiences so deeply, with its sweet love story, appealing stars, and sympathetic look at the difficulties of a returning soldier.

driven by compassion as they open up their home, and the season is conducive to the forgiveness at the heart of the story.

Toward the end, Shirley Temple plays an emotional scene with Ginger Rogers that created a major production issue. Dieterle originally shot the scene favoring Rogers and eliminating some of Temple's dialogue. When Selznick saw the rough cut, he was not pleased and rewrote the scene himself. Then he brought in director George Cukor to reshoot Temple's

Over plum pudding, Tom Tully leads his family and Joseph Cotten in a Christmas carol.

Holiday Moment

On Christmas Eve, Spring Byington carries a flaming plum pudding into the dining room, and everyone proceeds to sing "O Come, All Ye Faithful" around the table. The warmth and simplicity of this moment come off as a touching slice of 1940s home-front life.

A COLUMNIST MASQUERADING
AS A PROFESSIONAL HOMEMAKER
IS IN A PICKLE WHEN SHE
MUST PREPARE AND HOST A
PERFECT CHRISTMAS DINNER—IN A
CONNECTICUT FARMHOUSE SHE
DOESN'T HAVE.

Director
PETER GODFREY

Producer
WILLIAM JACOBS

Screenplay
LIONEL HOUSER and ADELE COMANDINI, from an
original story by AILEEN HAMILTON

Starring

BARBARA STANWYCK	Elizabeth Lane
DENNIS MORGAN	Jefferson Jones
SYDNEY GREENSTREET	Alexander Yardley
REGINALD GARDINER	John Sloan
S. Z. SAKALL	Felix
ROBERT SHAYNE	Dudley Beecham
UNA O'CONNOR	Norah
JOYCE COMPTON	Mary Lee
DICK ELLIOTT	Judge Crowthers

Five years after the dramatic romance of *Remember the Night* (1940), Barbara Stanwyck starred in another holiday classic, *Christmas in Connecticut*, this time operating in cheerful farce mode. In the interim, she had appeared in ten other films, a mix of comedies and dramas that cemented her standing as one of Hollywood's most versatile actresses. The contrast was even more pronounced when measured against her preceding film, *Double Indemnity* (1944). In that suspenseful film noir, Stanwyck had played a murderous femme fatale; in *Christmas in Connecticut*, the suspense revolves around whether Stanwyck can successfully flip a pancake.

She plays a wildly popular magazine columnist named Elizabeth Lane, "America's Best Cook," essentially the Martha Stewart of the era. She's known as a model homemaker with

Dennis Morgan sings to Barbara Stanwyck on Christmas Eve.

Dennis Morgan watches Barbara Stanwyck try to tend to the baby.

perfect recipes and domestic tips, and she has a loving husband, an eight-month-old baby, and an idyllic Connecticut farmhouse. The only problem? It's all a sham. Elizabeth actually lives alone in a Manhattan apartment without so much as a window box. She can't cook toast, much less roast a goose. She's been borrowing recipes from a Hungarian chef known as Uncle Felix and otherwise conjuring her columns out of thin air. Her publisher is not in on the ruse, which means that when he compels her, in a PR move, to host a wounded sailor for Christmas, she has to scramble to come up with a husband, baby, and Connecticut farmhouse fast or risk losing her job. Complicating matters are the sparks that fly between Elizabeth and the

sailor—and the publisher inviting himself to Connecticut, too!

Stanwyck's sincerity makes lines like "When you're kissing me, don't talk about plumbing" all the funnier. She also brings impeccable physical timing to a sequence where she fumbles with a baby, not knowing how to give it a bath. Luckily, the sailor does. He can even handle a cloth diaper, much to Elizabeth's delight.

He's played by Dennis Morgan, then approaching the peak of his stardom. Warner Bros. was using him in many genres, including musicals and westerns, and during the war years he had become extremely popular. A 1945 magazine article noted: "When Warner Brothers suddenly awoke to the fact that Dennis Morgan was receiving more fan mail than any star on the lot, no one was more surprised than they. They hadn't realized he was a big star. . . . His entire career is built on a series of mild successes." In fact, Morgan briefly became the highest-paid actor at the studio. His fine voice made him especially likable in musicals, and even *Christmas in Connecticut* works in a song for him, "The Wish That I Wish Tonight." After this picture became the second major hit in a row for Morgan— after *God Is My Co-Pilot* (1945)—a pleased Warner executive described him as "another Van Johnson," a reference to the amiable MGM star

ABOVE: S. Z. Sakall teaches Barbara Stanwyck how to flip a flapjack.

RIGHT: Reginald Gardiner and Sydney Greenstreet have a Christmas drink.

Robert Shayne, Reginald Gardiner, S. Z. Sakall, and Barbara Stanwyck hatch a plan.

The farmhouse here, designed by art director Stanley Fleischer, is a wonder: spacious, beautifully decorated, warmly lit, at once modern and quaint, and accessible by horse-drawn sleigh. It's wholly inviting, and somehow the cavernous living room is kept perfectly heated by a marvel of a fireplace. ("I specialize in fireplaces," proclaims Gardiner, as Stanwyck's architect friend and would-be husband.) The effect is to contribute to the slight fantasy aspect of the film as a whole and to the sentimental idea of a snowy Connecticut farm being the ideal place to celebrate Christmas.

On August 8, 1945—the height of summer—Warner Bros. threw an elaborate premiere for the film in Norwalk, Connecticut, complete with a Christmas parade that drew 20,000 spectators. There was even a party with yuletide trimmings for GIs who had been overseas during the previous Christmas and were about to be redeployed. As it turned out, the war would end one month later.

Christmas in Connecticut became one of Warner Bros.' biggest hits of the year but only grew into a holiday perennial decades later, thanks to repeat television airings. While not quite a staple, like *It's a Wonderful Life* or *Miracle on 34th Street*, it has an endearing screwball charm all its own.

then ranked as the number-two box office draw in all of Hollywood.

The supporting cast offers comic delights, including two rotund *Casablanca* (1942) alumni, S. Z. "Cuddles" Sakall, endearing as always, and Sydney Greenstreet in a rare comedy role. Reginald Gardiner inexplicably keeps a hand in his pocket in virtually every scene, even when bounding up the stairs, and character actors Dick Elliott and Una O'Connor bring zest to their roles of judge and cook.

Christmas in Connecticut is one of many holiday movies to turn a house into a "star."

Holiday Moment

The image of Dennis Morgan singing at the piano while Barbara Stanwyck decorates the tree is about as Christmassy as could be, but there's another moment that defines the season even more poignantly: the square dance. In a town hall done up with holiday decorations and a Christmas tree, a large crowd dances joyfully and buys war bonds—a reminder that for all the breezy comedy, this is still very much a film of the war era. At one point, Reginald Gardiner playfully swoops in to dance a step with Stanwyck, and her reaction—trying to conceal a laugh—seems genuine and spontaneous. It's a lovely moment in a scene of community togetherness that feels as if it could be happening in any American town at Christmas during World War II.

The Christmas dance

IT'S A WONDERFUL LIFE

RKO/Liberty Films, 1946
Black and White, 130 minutes

**A MAN ON THE VERGE OF SUICIDE
IS GIVEN THE CHANCE TO
SEE WHAT THE WORLD WOULD BE LIKE
HAD HE NEVER BEEN BORN.**

Director and Producer
FRANK CAPRA

Screenplay
FRANCES GOODRICH, ALBERT HACKETT, FRANK CAPRA,
and JO SWERLING, based on a story by
PHILIP VAN DOREN STERN

Starring

JAMES STEWART	George Bailey
DONNA REED	Mary Hatch
LIONEL BARRYMORE	Mr. Potter
THOMAS MITCHELL	Uncle Billy
HENRY TRAVERS	Clarence
BEULAH BONDI	Mrs. Bailey
FRANK FAYLEN	Ernie
WARD BOND	Bert
GLORIA GRAHAME	Violet
H. B. WARNER	Mr. Gower
TODD KARNS	Harry Bailey
SAMUEL S. HINDS	Pa Bailey
FRANK ALBERTSON	Sam Wainwright
LILLIAN RANDOLPH	Annie
SHELDON LEONARD	Nick
CHARLES LANE	Real Estate Salesman
CAROL COOMBS	Janie
KAROLYN GRIMES	Zuzu
JIMMY HAWKINS	Tommy

Frank Capra's masterpiece is also the ultimate Christmas movie. Set on Christmas Eve as a man, George Bailey, contemplates suicide, *It's a Wonderful Life* uses flashbacks to take the audience through the events of George's life—the joys and the letdowns—that have brought him to this moment. Then, thanks to a guardian angel named Clarence who hasn't yet earned his wings, George is afforded "a great gift": a chance to see what the world would be like without him.

By this point, all audience members have likely recognized themselves in George Bailey to some degree—perhaps in his frustration over roads not taken, or his disillusionment over dreams unrealized, or his doubts about the importance of his daily life. As a result, when George realizes how much he has touched the lives of others and renews his will to live, his sheer joy becomes the audience's joy, an affirmation that simple acts of kindness, generosity, and selflessness count

BELOW: Henry Travers, as Clarence, starts to convince James Stewart of the alternate reality. **OPPOSITE:** James Stewart and Donna Reed after the school dance-turned-swimfest. Perfectly cast, Reed made the film on loan-out from MGM.

The ageless Mr. Potter (Lionel Barrymore, seated) with Frank Hagney, Bobby Anderson as young George, and Samuel S. Hinds as Pa Bailey

for everything in this world. *It's a Wonderful Life* is two Christmas movies in one: an honest depiction of alienation that the holiday magnifies for some people, and a heartfelt expression of what others consider to be the season's ideal meaning.

The film derived from a short story by Philip Van Doren Stern called "The Greatest Gift." When Stern couldn't find a publisher, he printed some copies himself and sent them out as Christmas cards, including one to his Hollywood agent—who promptly sold the story to

RKO. After several failed attempts at a screenplay, RKO sold the property to Frank Capra, who loved it for its whimsy and its darkness, which he felt was right for the less-innocent postwar climate.

The story's blend of tones and emotions was right up Capra's alley: fantasy and reality, comedy and drama, romance and bitterness are all believably in the mix. The alternate-reality sequence is so disturbing that it feels like a horror movie shot in film noir style; it's a powerful shock to the senses for a movie remembered primarily for its

James Stewart in private anguish as Donna Reed and the kids trim the tree

humor and joyfulness. Capra later said the most challenging balancing act came when he directed George losing his temper at home with his kids: "It's a very dramatic scene, and yet, it can get laughs," he recounted. "Which do you want it to do? . . . If it becomes too funny, [they'll] laugh at the drama, too."

James Stewart's magnificent performance also captures that balancing act. He ages believably over twenty-seven story years, and he is as credible as a romantic husband and kindhearted father as he is a tormented soul, frustrated at being stuck in Bedford Falls running the Bailey Building and Loan. Some of his darker moments are truly upsetting, as when he encounters the "alternate" Mary (Donna Reed) in the fantasy sequence or berates Uncle Billy (Thomas Mitchell) for losing $8,000. For all his exuberant comedy and playfulness—and *It's a Wonderful Life* contains plenty—Stewart shows dark emotions on-screen to a degree he never had before. That paved the way for even more traumatized and obsessive characters he would play in thrillers and westerns for directors Alfred Hitchcock and Anthony Mann, respectively.

Among the excellent supporting players are two who provide other Christmas movie connections. Beulah Bondi had played Fred MacMurray's mom in *Remember the Night* (1940), and here she plays Stewart's lovable mother for the fourth time in her career—with a fifth still to come on television twenty-five years later. Lionel Barrymore depicts one of the great screen villains in Mr. Potter, a Scrooge-like character in a tale that has much in common with *A Christmas Carol*. Barrymore, in fact, played Ebenezer Scrooge on radio broadcasts every holiday season for the last twenty years of his life. He was meant to play Scrooge in the 1938 film version but an injury prevented it, and he was confined to a wheelchair from then on. His performance here is a glimpse of what his Scrooge might have been like.

It's a Wonderful Life received positive reviews but fell short at the box office. It was nominated for five Academy Awards, including Best Picture, Director, and Actor, but won none. It seemed destined for obscurity until the 1970s, when it fell into the public domain and began saturating television screens every December. Audiences rediscovered it, and the film grew into a national phenomenon and recognized classic. It's as if individual movie lovers came to the film's rescue because of all the joy it had given them—just as George Bailey's friends do for him.

James Stewart with Bill Edmunds (left) and Stanley Andrews (right), as George falls to his deepest despair at a bar on Christmas Eve

ABOVE LEFT: Producer-director Frank Capra with James Stewart ABOVE RIGHT: James Stewart as George Bailey, redeemed and with family OPPOSITE: "Merry Christmas, Bedford Falls!"

Holiday Moment

George Bailey's reunion with his family and friends is one of the most joyous endings in movies. Stewart's complete physical commitment to the scene makes it indelible, and the screenplay and direction have skillfully built the drama to this moment of release, but the Christmas Eve setting is also a vital factor. The goodwill, generosity, and togetherness of loved ones that make up the heart of the scene are all aspects of the season, and Capra links them to Christmas by prominently including a Christmas tree and the singing of a carol. When a ringing bell on the tree soon gives way to the ringing bell of the Liberty Films logo, the moment also becomes linked to Frank Capra himself, and his optimistic sense of humanity.

MIRACLE ON 34th STREET

20th Century-Fox, 1947 • Black and White, 96 minutes

A DEPARTMENT STORE
SANTA CLAUS CLAIMS TO BE THE
REAL THING.

Director
GEORGE SEATON

Producer
WILLIAM PERLBERG

Screenplay
GEORGE SEATON, based on a story
by VALENTINE DAVIES

Starring

MAUREEN O'HARA	Doris Walker
JOHN PAYNE	Fred Gailey
EDMUND GWENN	Kris Kringle
GENE LOCKHART	Judge Henry X. Harper
NATALIE WOOD	Susan Walker
PORTER HALL	Granville Sawyer
WILLIAM FRAWLEY	Charlie Halloran
JEROME COWAN	District Attorney Thomas Mara

One of the most beloved of Christmas movies, *Miracle on 34th Street* taps into a cherished rite of childhood—believing in Santa Claus—with charm, humor, and playfulness to spare, all leavened by a healthy dose of cynicism. At the heart of the film is the relationship between a man named Kris Kringle (Edmund Gwenn), who says he's Santa, and a little girl named Susan (Natalie Wood), who does not believe in Santa because her mother has taught her such things are "silly." But as the story unfolds, Susan starts to wonder—and so does the audience.

Miracle on 34th Street contains not a single frame of anything fantastical: no flying sled, no elves, no acts of magic or the supernatural. Nothing is ever shown on-screen that could not be explained logically, and most of the production was even filmed on location

Edmund Gwenn with a skeptical Natalie Wood

Natalie Wood and John Payne as the real Macy's parade goes by on Central Park West

in New York, greatly enhancing the realism. Even so, the movie works simultaneously as realism and fantasy, with any fantasy happening completely inside the minds of viewers who believe Kris to be Santa and not just "a nice old man with whiskers."

It wasn't originally envisioned this way. Valentine Davies conceived his story out of concern over the commercialism of Christmas, and his first idea was for outright fantasy: to show Santa Claus at his North Pole workshop before journeying to New York to somehow confront the commercialism. Writer-director George Seaton suggested it might be better if the tale were about a man who *thought* he was Santa Claus, with the audience wondering if it were true.

They outlined a story called *This Is the Time* and took it to Fox studio chief Darryl Zanuck in 1945. "Who the hell is going to care about an old man who thinks he's Santa Claus?" Zanuck exclaimed. Davies and Seaton then thought to make the man a Macy's department store Santa, and the story fell into place because now they could come up with clear reasons for other characters—and the audience—to "care."

Through that evolution, the screenplay changed titles (to *The Big Heart*, *Kris Kringle*, *It's Only Human*, and, finally, *Miracle on 34th Street*) but kept its satirical jabs at holiday commercialism. Beyond driving Kris's motivations ("Christmas and I are sort of getting lost in the shuffle," he observes), it's the basis for a key plot turn, after Kris gets into trouble for steering customers to Gimbels when Macy's doesn't have what they want. (He had been instructed to push other Macy's products, but to Santa, of course, that wouldn't be fair to the children.) It's also the basis for wry comedy, as when R. H. Macy decides to apply Kris's idea company-wide. "We'll be known as . . . the store with a heart," he says, "the store that places public service ahead of profit. And consequently, we'll make more profits than ever before."

In fact, what makes the movie so satisfying is that its meaning derives as much from irony

Santa on trial, with Jerome Cowan, Gene Lockhart, and Edmund Gwenn

and cynicism as it does from sentiment. At one point, Kris is placed into the Bellevue mental ward—a dastardly thing to do to this gentle, loving Santa Claus! When he is put on trial in an attempt to prove his derangement, the film brings all its ideas together in an ingeniously written sequence that concocts perfectly logical reasons to find him both guilty *and* innocent. Jerome Cowan's district attorney finds his own arguments hilariously stifled by his love for his son, and Gene Lockhart's judge endures amusing political pressures, all of which add more layers of cynicism couched in comedy.

Seaton filmed in as many real locations as possible and insisted on using the Macy's and

Maureen O'Hara and John Payne have differing ideas when it comes to kids and Santa.

Gimbels names. The Fox legal department told him the stores would never approve, but Seaton went to New York and lobbied their chiefs personally. He filmed inside Macy's, mostly after hours, and not just in the showrooms; the employees' cafeteria, corridors, elevator, and locker room all appear on-screen.

Macy's and the city of New York also granted permission to shoot the 1946 Macy's Thanksgiving Day Parade for the opening sequence, in which Kris is drafted off the street to replace a sloshed Santa (Percy Helton in an amusing bit). These shots began the film's production, with Seaton using fourteen cameras

stationed along the route. Maureen O'Hara, who plays Natalie Wood's mother and the Macy's executive in charge of the parade, later said, "It was bitterly cold that day, and Edmund and I envied Natalie and John Payne, who were watching the parade from a window."

O'Hara was glad to be working for a third time with Payne, whose role here, as a neighbor of Wood and O'Hara's who ends up representing Gwenn in the trial, was his own career favorite. He tried for years to get a sequel made, even writing a screenplay himself, but it was not to be. Natalie Wood was eight years old, and this was her fifth picture in a fast-growing career. Partway through production, she started work on another film, *The Ghost and Mrs. Muir* (1947), and for a time she was even working on three pictures simultaneously. She impressed everyone with her professionalism and sophistication, memorizing the entire script and often delivering her lines flawlessly on the first take. "She was so business-like, she amazed me," Seaton said. Off the set, Wood called O'Hara "Mama Maureen" and O'Hara called her "little old lady" because she seemed so beyond her years.

In one regard, Wood was still a typical little girl: she believed that Edmund Gwenn *was* Santa Claus. "I guess I had an inkling that *maybe* it wasn't so," she recalled, "but I . . . had never

Christmas morning is even better with the real(?) Santa Claus.

seen him without his beard—because he used to come in early in the morning and spend several hours putting on this wonderful beard and mustache. And at the end of the shoot, when we had a set party, I saw this strange man, without the beard, and I just couldn't get it together."

Kris Kringle was the role of a lifetime for Gwenn. The sixty-nine-year-old longtime char-

acter actor threw himself into the part, even putting on significant weight which he was never able to fully shed. He is utterly convincing as a man who believes he is Santa Claus and pitch-perfect *as* Santa, not just physically or because of the twinkle in his eye but in the kindness and empathy he brings to his performance. When he accepted the Academy Award

Maureen O'Hara called Natalie Wood her favorite movie daughter.

for Best Supporting Actor, he said, "Now I *know* there's a Santa Claus."

Miracle on 34th Street won two further Oscars, for Story and Screenplay, and was nominated for Best Picture, but in early 1947, Fox

could foresee none of this. The studio was so worried about the film's prospects that a release date was set not for December but for the beginning of the summer movie season, when overall attendance was higher. The advertising didn't even mention Christmas. But the movie was a classic sleeper, seeming to come out of nowhere to fine reviews and large crowds. Fans sent letters to Fox addressed to Santa Claus. Gimbels took out a full-page ad congratulating Macy's, and both stores for a time instituted policies of redirecting customers to the other store as needed.

Ultimately, the picture has endured perhaps most because it incorporates the audience's own nostalgia into the storytelling: to believe in Kris Kringle is to revisit one's own Christmas past, and in that sense, *Miracle on 34th Street* is one of the purest Christmas movies of all.

Holiday Moment

When Kris slips into perfect Dutch to converse and sing with a lonely little Dutch orphan, even the coldest of hearts will melt. It's one of the nearest moments to fantasy in the movie because it gives the impression that Kris could speak fluently in any language to any kid in the world—and wouldn't the one and only Santa Claus have that ability?

Director
HENRY KOSTER

Producer
SAMUEL GOLDWYN

Screenplay
ROBERT E. SHERWOOD and LEONARDO BERCOVICI,
from the novel by ROBERT NATHAN

Starring

CARY GRANT..........................Dudley
LORETTA YOUNG ....Julia Brougham
DAVID NIVEN..............Henry Brougham
MONTY WOOLLEY ......Professor Wutheridge
JAMES GLEASON.................Sylvester
GLADYS COOPER ....Mrs. Hamilton
ELSA LANCHESTER ....Matilda

**AN ANGEL COMES TO EARTH
TO HELP A BISHOP REGAIN HIS WAY,
BUT HE FALLS FOR THE BISHOP'S
WIFE IN THE PROCESS.**

One year after Clarence the angel showed up to help George Bailey in *It's a Wonderful Life* (1946), Dudley the angel arrived to help Henry Brougham, a bishop losing sight of what matters in his life as he struggles to fund a new cathedral. Like Clarence, Dudley is an answer to a prayer, doesn't have wings, talks up to the heavens, and can appear or disappear in an instant. Unlike Clarence, he's experienced in helping humans, plays the harp beautifully, ice skates like an Olympian, and is dapper—*very* dapper. He is, after all, played by Cary Grant.

Every woman he meets finds him beguiling, and when it comes to Henry's wife, Julia, the attraction is dangerously mutual.

The charm of Cary Grant pretty well defines the charm of *The Bishop's Wife*, a warm-hearted fantasy that culminates on Christmas and is sure to put anyone in a cheery holiday mood. It's so smoothly entertaining that it's a surprise to discover how troubled its production was. Filming started in February 1947 with Grant playing the bishop, Niven playing the angel, and William Seiter directing. After

Cary Grant's angel has his work cut out trying to repair the bishop's marriage.

three weeks, producer Samuel Goldwyn shut the picture down, unhappy with the footage so far. He replaced Seiter with Henry Koster and decided the film would be better if Grant and Niven switched roles. Grant did not want to play the angel and even asked to be let go from the film, but Goldwyn refused. For several weeks, Koster worked with Robert Sherwood on revising the script to allow for the casting change, and Goldwyn had several sets torn down and rebuilt from scratch, sparing no expense. (At some point in the process, Goldwyn also brought on ace writers Billy Wilder and Charles Brackett to polish some scenes, uncredited.)

Goldwyn was known as a meticulous, hands-on producer with impeccable taste down to the smallest details—a quality that had served him well. During the production break, in fact, his previous film, *The Best Years of Our Lives* (1946), won the Oscar for Best Picture, and Goldwyn himself won the prestigious Irving G. Thalberg Award—for the second time in his career. At this moment, he was truly the toast of Hollywood, and his moves on *The Bishop's Wife* were proving to be astute. Filming restarted with a cast not exactly thrilled about all the delays and changes, but to their credit, they delivered wonderful performances under

Radiant Loretta Young in the "hardest part" she ever played

Koster's direction. Loretta Young (a major star too little remembered today) said the role of the neglected wife was the "hardest part I'd ever played." Koster had her underplay her scenes in order to keep the film's tone away from melodrama, and Young said "that's why it was so hard—I had to avoid doing anything."

True to Koster's instincts, the movie feels whimsical with touches of seriousness, not melodramatic. Elsa Lanchester's housekeeper can barely contain her attraction to Cary

TOP: Monty Woolley with Loretta Young and his Christmas tree, for which he paid "ten cents a branch."

BOTTOM LEFT: Denzel Washington and Whitney Houston in the 1996 remake, *The Preacher's Wife.*

BOTTOM RIGHT: Bishop David Niven and angel Cary Grant. They had begun filming in the opposite roles before switching and starting over.

Grant's Dudley whenever he is around, and Dudley himself is endlessly playful. He tosses papers in the air and they fly into their proper files; he gives Monty Woolley's sherry bottle the power of always staying full; and he helps a little girl wallop a boy with a snowball by magically improving its trajectory. That last scene is especially fun because the girl is played by Karolyn Grimes, who had played George Bailey's daughter Zuzu in *It's a Wonderful Life*, and the boy is played by Bobby Anderson, who had played George Bailey as a kid.

Woolley provides another Christmas movie link with his broken-down scholar recalling Sheridan Whiteside, his character in *The Man Who Came to Dinner* (1942). And there's a touch of Christmas in the marvelous performance by Gladys Cooper as a wealthy widow who undergoes a Scrooge-like transformation. The constant snow, decorations, and story centered on treating people with kindness and compassion all lend a distinct holiday glow.

The humor and charm were not enough, however, to make the film an instant winner at the box office. Despite excellent reviews, audiences stayed away until Goldwyn figured out that the title was making people think the movie was strongly religious, or at least too tame. The canny producer changed the title mid-release

Cary Grant plays a charming scene with Karolyn Grimes (Zuzu in *It's a Wonderful Life*), as Sara Haden, Loretta Young, and David Niven look on. The striking composition was by cameraman Gregg Toland (best known for his work on *Citizen Kane*).

in some markets to *Cary and the Bishop's Wife*, making it sound more mischievous, and ticket sales indeed shot up.

The movie was nominated for five Academy Awards, including Best Picture and Director, and it won for Sound. Loretta Young, however, did win Best Actress that year—for *The Farmer's Daughter* (1947). She went on to work with Henry Koster once more, on *Come to the Stable* (1949), another Christmastime favorite, and was again nominated.

Cary Grant enjoying his handiwork

Holiday Moment

One of Cary Grant's most charming moments comes when Dudley decorates a Christmas tree with a few waves of his hand. This may or may not take the fun out of the task, but certainly anyone would want Dudley around to "un-decorate" the tree!

3 GODFATHERS

MGM, 1948 • Color, 106 minutes

Director

JOHN FORD

Producer

MERIAN C. COOPER [uncredited]

Screenplay

LAURENCE STALLINGS and FRANK S. NUGENT,
from the story by PETER B. KYNE

Starring

JOHN WAYNE	Robert Marmaduke Sangster Hightower
PEDRO ARMENDARIZ	Pedro Roca Fuerte
HARRY CAREY JR.	William Kearney
WARD BOND	Perley "Buck" Sweet
MAE MARSH	Mrs. Perley Sweet
MILDRED NATWICK	The Mother
JANE DARWELL	Miss Florie
GUY KIBBEE	The Judge
DOROTHY FORD	Ruby Latham
BEN JOHNSON	Member of Posse
CHARLES HALTON	Oliver Latham
HANK WORDEN	Curly

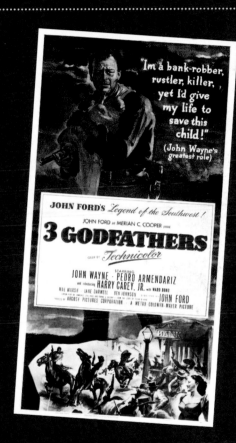

ON THE RUN FROM A SHERIFF,
THREE BANK ROBBERS RESCUE
A BABY AND ATTEMPT TO GET HIM TO
SAFETY ACROSS A DESERT.

The three godfathers: Harry Carey Jr., John Wayne, and Pedro Armendariz

3 Godfathers begins as a straightforward western. A few days before Christmas, three men rob a bank and escape into the desert, with scant water and just two horses. A sheriff sets out to catch them, anticipating which of the few nearby water sources they might ride to, and a suspenseful battle of wits ensues. Then everything shifts. The robbers come upon a covered wagon holding a woman about to give birth. They deliver the baby, promise the dying mother that they will see him to safety, and proceed on foot across miles of desert toward the town of New Jerusalem, using a star to guide them. The sheriff is still in pursuit, but the robbers are now focused on saving that child—as well as their own redemption. The story has transformed into a parable of the Three Wise Men.

Published in 1913 by Peter B. Kyne, this sentimental allegory had already been the basis for four movies. The second version, *Marked Men* (1919), had starred Harry Carey and been directed by John Ford, who considered it his favorite of his silent work. (Sadly, no prints are known to exist.) Ford became one of the great Hollywood directors and Carey became a major star, and the pair collaborated on more than two dozen other westerns. When Carey died in 1947, Ford decided to honor his old friend by making a new version of the story with a leading role for twenty-seven-year-old Harry Carey Jr., known to all as "Dobe" for his adobe-red hair. The resulting film has the feel of a nostalgic family affair, with an opening dedication, "To the Memory of Harry Carey, Bright Star of the early western sky," followed a few seconds later by the credit, "introducing Harry Carey Jr." It didn't matter that Dobe had already racked up four previous acting credits.

It also didn't matter that he had grown up knowing the cantankerous John Ford as

Harry Carey Jr.'s death scene—"the toughest day of my motion picture life"

"Uncle Jack." There would be no kid gloves on the set just because of their close history. The day they shot his death scene, Carey later wrote, was "the toughest day of my motion picture life." They were filming in torrid Death Valley, California, in triple-digit heat. After the first take, an unhappy Ford chewed Carey out before ordering the entire crew to walk away. "Let him lay out there in the sun for a while and think about the goddamned scene," Ford said. After half an hour, Carey recounted, "My mouth got so dry I couldn't swallow. My back was on fire. That salt flat

ABOVE: Led by Ward Bond, the posse reaches the desert camp.

RIGHT: Guy Kibbee in his final film role as the judge (left), John Wayne (center), and Ward Bond (hat in hand), with studio lights visible above

was so hot I felt I was in a frying pan." Ford and the crew returned, and they shot the scene again, with Armendariz kneeling beside Carey and John Wayne holding up his hat to shade Carey's face. This time, "It wasn't me talking. I heard a voice I'd never heard before, the voice of a dying young man. Who was this? It was like I was outside myself." Carey finished the scene, and Wayne lifted him up. "Uncle Jack" smiled and took Carey's face in his hands. "Why didn't you do that the first time?" he asked. "See how easy it was?"

This picture is underrated in Ford's career, partly because he made it between two much bigger films, *Fort Apache* (1948) and *She Wore a Yellow Ribbon* (1949), giving it the air of an understated, minor work. It has many wonderful things going for it beyond its Christmas allegory, including delightful turns from Ward Bond, Mae Marsh, and Jane Darwell, who's a hoot as a man-crazy pioneer woman, and stunning photography from Winton Hoch that enhances the heartfelt tone. This was Hoch's first time working with John Ford; he would later shoot *The Searchers* (1956), one of Ford's most ravishing films.

3 Godfathers has some interesting connections to other holiday movies. The comical

An intense John Wayne trying to stay alive

image of John Wayne floundering with a baby, not knowing the first thing to do, recalls Barbara Stanwyck's baby-fumbling in *Christmas in Connecticut* (1945). Then there's the odd Christmas-film symmetry of the two Harry Careys. At age sixty-one, Harry Carey Sr. played one of the three leading men in *Beyond Tomorrow* (1940), last seen as a spirit making his way to an afterlife; *3 Godfathers* is dedicated to his memory and stars his son as one of *its* three leading men; and at age sixty-two, Harry Carey Jr. would take a small role in another Christmas classic—*Gremlins* (1984).

Holiday Moment

It's Christmas Eve in the town of New Jerusalem. The saloon is decorated for the holiday, full of townsfolk and piano music. In staggers John Wayne with the baby; he makes his way to the bar to order a milk and a beer, and everything stops as the baby becomes the center of attention. For a few moments, there is no sheriff's posse on his tail or any trouble at all: just triumph and redemption, as the piano player starts "Silent Night."

The New Jerusalem saloon on Christmas Eve. The pianist is played by Richard Hageman, the film's composer. At far left is Gertrude Astor in an uncredited bit; she had starred with Harry Carey Sr. in a 1917 two-reel western directed by John Ford.

HOLIDAY AFFAIR

RKO, 1949 • Black and White, 87 minutes

Director
DON HARTMAN

Producer
DON HARTMAN

Screenplay
ISOBEL LENNART, based on the
story "Christmas Gift" by JOHN D. WEAVER

Starring

ROBERT MITCHUM....................Steve
JANET LEIGH.......................Connie
WENDELL COREY......................Carl
GORDON GEBERT.....................Timmy
GRIFF BARNETT..................Mr. Ennis
ESTHER DALE ....Mrs. Ennis
HENRY O'NEILL ....Mr. Crowley
HENRY MORGAN ....Police Lieutenant

**A WAR WIDOW WITH A YOUNG SON
IS COURTED BY TWO MEN.**

"You'll like him in a new type of role!" proclaimed the trailers for *Holiday Affair*. The reference was to Robert Mitchum, but in truth it was the same old "Mitchum" in a new type of *movie*. Yes, he is first seen here as an unlikely sales clerk, sure to draw chuckles from anyone used to seeing him in tough film noir, but he nonetheless brings his distinct rebel attitude to this light comedy-drama. His character, Steve, could easily have wandered in from *Out of the Past* (1947), leaving behind his gun but keeping the frank talk and seduction skills. Even his casual first line of dialogue—"All right, gentlemen, what do we do now?"—could have been spoken to a roomful of hoodlums.

In fact, he's addressing a horde of young boys while demonstrating a toy train—one of a series of jobs he's taken to save money for a boat-building venture. The story quickly focuses on his growing Christmastime romance with Connie Ennis (Janet Leigh), a war widow with a little boy named Timmy (Gordon Gebert) and an amorous lawyer friend named Carl (Wendell Corey, lending dignity to a thankless role). Connie finds herself pulled between Steve and Carl while unable to let go of the memory of her

---

PREVIOUS PAGE: Gordon Gebert is one happy kid when Robert Mitchum is around.
BELOW: Janet Leigh's two choices: Wendell Corey (left) and Robert Mitchum

When *Holiday Affair* fizzled at the box office, RKO tried a new tack, replacing the jaunty advertising with a more hard-edged look.

husband, a plot element that gives the movie a tinge of postwar melancholy.

Based on a story called "Christmas Gift" and filmed under the title *The Man Who Played Santa Claus*, *Holiday Affair* was produced and directed for RKO by Don Hartman, best known as a writer of Paramount comedies, including many with Bob Hope or Bing Crosby. He can be seen in a cameo early on, exiting a phone booth past Janet Leigh.

RKO no doubt made *Holiday Affair* as an attempt to capitalize on Fox's *Miracle on 34th Street* (1947): both films are set in New York, make prominent use of department stores, have the store owners as characters, and incorporate romances involving single working mothers. Both also devote much attention to their child actors, but while *Miracle* is geared toward the child in all of us and touches on fantasy, *Holiday Affair* is aimed more at adults. Even little Timmy Ennis, while cute and spunky, is embroiled in the churn of adult-relationship issues as he confronts the prospect of a new stepfather. As Steve observes, Connie has turned Timmy into sort of a substitute husband, offhandedly calling him "Mr. Ennis."

Many of Leigh's scenes with Gebert feel natural and unscripted, and her chemistry with

TOP: A happy
Gordon Gebert
on Christmas morning

BOTTOM: The pivotal
dinner scene, a staple of
Christmas movies

Robert Mitchum mans the toy department.

Mitchum is just as appealing. It was an early starring role for Leigh, then twenty-two and on loan from MGM, and other than having to endure RKO chief Howard Hughes's unwanted advances, she remembered this picture fondly. She adored Robert Mitchum, describing him as "the most liberated spirit I had ever come across." The first time she ever saw him, he was walking out of his dressing room on the RKO lot playing a saxophone, with an entourage of people trailing behind. One scene called for Mitchum to approach Leigh from behind and turn her around for a small surprise kiss. Instead, he surprised her with a *big* kiss—"in a way that you would never do on a first date," Leigh recounted. "I was so shocked I couldn't speak."

Holiday Affair is full of charming set pieces, such as Mitchum's lunch date with Leigh in front of the Central Park seals, during which he feeds an "orphan" squirrel, as well as the amusing hearing in front of a befuddled police lieutenant (Henry Morgan). The picture was shot in the

Henry Morgan shines as an exasperated police lieutenant.

early 1949, he had served fifty days in prison for marijuana possession, an event that drew enormous interest, and now everyone wanted to see the so-called "dope addict." Upon his release, he famously told reporters that "jail is like Palm Springs without the riffraff," then returned to RKO to finish shooting *The Big Steal* (1949) and begin work on *Holiday Affair*.

The Big Steal was a summer hit, but *Holiday Affair* was a box-office dud. Even a shift in advertising strategy was too little, too late. Today, seasonal television airings have rescued the picture from oblivion, and it stands as a pleasant comedy with heartfelt charm and a good deal of holiday "glow" that makes the characters especially sympathetic. As one review said at the time, "You'll leave the theater glad you're alive and the world is peopled with such nice human beings."

summer of 1949 and rushed through postproduction to open in New York the day before Thanksgiving. The urgency wasn't as much due to the holiday theme as it was to take advantage of the heat surrounding Robert Mitchum. In

Holiday Moment

When Timmy feels guilty about having received an expensive Christmas present from out-of-work Steve, he steals off to Crowley's department store to try and return it. The seven-year-old finagles his way past stern guards and a compassionate secretary to the office of Mr. Crowley himself (who in a forward-looking comic touch is on his "meditation hour"). A little kid innocently pleading his case at Christmas in order to do a good deed is enough to tear at anyone's heartstrings—be it Mr. Crowley's or the audience's.

TRAIL OF ROBIN HOOD

Republic, 1950 • Color, 67 minutes

Director
WILLIAM WITNEY

Associate Producer
EDWARD J. WHITE

Screenplay
GERALD GERAGHTY

Starring

ROY ROGERS . . . . Roy Rogers
TRIGGER, THE SMARTEST
HORSE IN THE MOVIES . . . . Trigger
PENNY EDWARDS . . . . Toby Aldridge
GORDON JONES . . . . .Splinters McGonigle
JACK HOLT . . . . Jack Holt
REX ALLEN
ALLAN "ROCKY" LANE
MONTE HALE
WILLIAM FARNUM
TOM TYLER
RAY "CRASH" CORRIGAN
KERMIT MAYNARD
TOM KEENE
GEORGE CHESEBRO . . . . Themselves
EMORY PARNELL . . . . J. Corwin Aldridge
CAROL NUGENT . . . . Sis McGonigle
THE RIDERS OF THE
PURPLE SAGE . . . . Singing workers

ROY ROGERS AND TRIGGER INVESTIGATE A CASE OF CHRISTMAS TREE RUSTLING.

Christmas comes to the "B" western in *Trail of Robin Hood*. Unlike *3 Godfathers*, there's no allegory or deep meaning here—just sixty-seven minutes of wacky fun. The plot involves rival Christmas tree ranchers, with one, played by Jack Holt, deciding to sell his trees at cost as a way of doing a good holiday deed. This doesn't sit well with his rival, who turns to sabotage and even Christmas tree rustling in order to get his trees to market first. (The film has nothing to do with Robin Hood, although Holt is a vaguely Robin Hood–like character.) "King of the Cowboys" Roy Rogers is on hand as a government agent who aims to set things right—pausing, of course, for an occasional song. The best of these is "Every Day Is Christmas in the West," performed as Christmas dinner is being served on a day that isn't really Christmas, thanks to another quirky plot turn.

It's easy to forget just how popular Roy Rogers was at this time. According to annual surveys of movie theater owners, he was ranked in 1950 as the industry's top money-making western star—for the seventh consecutive year. For millions of kids at Saturday matinees, Roy and his horse Trigger were a reliable and reassuring screen presence; *Trail of Robin Hood* was one of six Rogers westerns to open in 1950 alone. Filmed in Trucolor, Republic Pictures' two-color process, and

shot around Big Bear Lake over one summer month, it was released just before Christmas.

Rogers's westerns had changed in recent years. There was now a greater emphasis on action than songs, largely because of William Witney. He had long ago carved a name for himself as perhaps the best director in town of serials, on such titles as *Adventures of Captain Marvel* (1941) and *Spy Smasher* (1942), and since 1946 he had been applying his fine pacing skills to all of Rogers's films. Witney,

---

PREVIOUS PAGE: Roy Rogers and Penny Edwards, who costarred because Roy's usual leading lady, wife Dale Evans, was about to give birth to their daughter. **BELOW:** Jack Holt welcomes Roy Rogers, astride Trigger, to his Christmas tree tying party.

Sabotage! Roy Rogers (the favorite cowboy star of *Die Hard*'s John McClane) rescues Jack Holt from a tree tying party gone ablaze.

in fact, is recognized as the originator of choreographing fights in bits and pieces to be assembled in the editing room—an idea he came up with after observing Busby Berkeley stage musical numbers at Warner Bros. *Trail of Robin Hood* feels almost like a miniserial, building to such set pieces as a runaway wagon, a burning building, and a burning bridge, where in true serial form the hero always averts disaster at just the last moment. All the while, the film delivers the easygoing comedy that Rogers's fans expect, right down to three scene-stealing animals: Trigger the horse, Bullet the dog, and a lovable turkey named Sir Galahad.

What makes the picture special for classic movie fans is its very "meta," or self-referential, quality. Roy Rogers had been playing screen characters named Roy Rogers for years, but here, old silent western star Jack Holt plays an old silent western star named Jack Holt, whose desire to thank his fans at Christmas is what drives the entire story line. "I made a little money in pictures and that's why I'm ranching," he says. "Every family that wants a tree is going to get one. I'm not interested in making a profit. If there is any,

ABOVE: A bevy of old cowboy stars help save the day. Foreground: Roy Rogers, Allan "Rocky" Lane, Monte Hale, Gordon Jones. Several more former stars in background.

RIGHT: Trigger, Penny Edwards, Roy Rogers, Bullet, and Gordon Jones console young Carol Nugent.

Foy Willing, Roy Rogers, and Penny Edwards await their Christmas turkey from Gordon Jones.

I'll give it to the children's home. Kids like that made it possible for me to become a star."

What's more, an entire brigade of past "B" western stars literally ride to Holt's rescue, as themselves: Allan Lane, Monte Hale, William Farnum, Kermit Maynard, Tom Keene, Tom Tyler, Ray Corrigan, and George Chesebro. (Chesebro, who was known for playing villains, is forced to promise that in this case he has good intentions.) The film also publi-cizes a fairly new Republic star, Rex Allen, by giving him a cameo.

That's the bizarre universe of *Trail of Robin Hood*: real life and movie life intermingle. Even the time period is a fantasy blend. The film looks and feels like a period western until cars, phones, and modern kitchens suddenly appear. But no one on-screen seems to mind, and neither will audiences of this cheerful Christmas entertainment.

A perfect Christmas moment: tying Christmas trees while singing a song, with a movie screen at the ready for an old western starring Jack Holt, who stands at far right

❧ *Holiday Moment* ❧

At Jack Holt's Christmas tree tying party, there's also tree trimming, a group sing-along ("Get a Christmas Tree for Johnny"), and finally a holiday tradition that anyone would love: screening an old film! Watching a classic movie at Christmas in which characters gather to watch a classic movie at Christmas—starring the character (Jack Holt) hosting the screening, who has essentially been playing himself the whole time—is the most intricately "meta" that a holiday movie moment could be.

SCROOGE
aka A CHRISTMAS CAROL

Renown Pictures, 1951 • Black and White, 86 minutes

Director

BRIAN DESMOND HURST

Producer

BRIAN DESMOND HURST

Screenplay

NOEL LANGLEY, adapted from
CHARLES DICKENS'S *A Christmas Carol*

Starring

ALASTAIR SIM . . . . Ebenezer Scrooge

KATHLEEN HARRISON . . . . Mrs. Dilber

MERVYN JOHNS . . . . Rob Cratchit

HERMIONE BADDELEY . . . . Mrs. Cratchit

MICHAEL HORDERN . . . . Jacob Marley

GEORGE COLE . . . . Young Ebenezer
Scrooge

JOHN CHARLESWORTH . . . . Peter Cratchit

ERNEST THESIGER . . . . Undertaker

GLYN DEARMAN . . . . Tiny Tim

PATRICK MACNEE . . . . Young Jacob Marley

A MISERLY MAN IS TAUGHT
THE MEANING OF CHRISTMAS BY
THREE SPIRITS WHO VISIT HIM
ON CHRISTMAS EVE.

Charles Dickens's tale of Ebenezer Scrooge, a crusty old miser transformed by the spirits of Christmas into a kind and compassionate man, has enthralled readers from the day it was published in 1843. It's also lent itself beautifully to the screen since at least 1901, when Daniel Smith starred in the six-minute *Scrooge, or Marley's Ghost*. Most recently, Christopher Plummer played Scrooge in *The Man Who Invented Christmas* (2017). In between, there have been far too many other versions to count, with *A Christmas Carol* adapted into dramas, comedies, musicals, westerns, animation, puppetry—virtually any variation possible, for the big screen and small. But there is one movie version that's just about perfect, the one against which all others must be measured: the 1951 *Scrooge*, made in England with Alastair Sim and released in the United States as *A Christmas Carol*.

Just as Edmund Gwenn has come to embody the popular conception of Santa Claus, thanks to *Miracle on 34th Street*, Alastair Sim is for many the definitive Scrooge. Dickens described the character as "hard and sharp as flint, from which no steel had ever struck out generous fire." Certainly Sim's sneering demeanor, his staccato gait, his cantankerous way of telling Bob Cratchit on Christmas Eve, "You want the whole *day* off tomorrow, I

suppose," are all indelible, but so are the complex dimensions he brings to his performance later on.

He draws sympathy, for instance, when he tells the Spirit of Christmas Yet to Come: "I fear you more than any other specter I've seen. But even in my fear I must tell you, I am too old! I cannot change!" Another Scrooge might have spoken those words with defiance; Sim expresses shame, sorrow, and resignation, not just with his voice but with his entire body language. On Christmas Day, when the transformed Scrooge asks his nephew's wife if she can "forgive a pig-headed old fool for having no eyes to see with, no ears to hear with," Sim makes one believe that this is somehow still the same character from the beginning, changed not into someone completely new so much as into the tender soul he always had buried within himself.

Remarkably, Sim's casting was highly controversial. He was already a popular star in England but was known for eccentric comedy characters, and many believed he didn't have the dramatic chops for Scrooge. There was enough of an outcry that George Minter, the managing director of Renown Pictures, wrote an article for *Picturegoer* magazine entitled "Why I Chose Sim"—two full months before the film even opened! He wrote, "Dickens obviously intended Scrooge to be a figure of fun, not of fustian melodrama," and he

Scrooge (Alastair Sim) with the Spirit of Christmas Past (Michael Dolan)

defended Sim as "a comedian and a brilliant all-round character actor."

Beyond Alastair Sim, *Scrooge* boasts an intelligent screenplay by Noel Langley that makes a few alterations to the story. For instance, the Christmas Past sequence is longer than in other versions because it drums up new context to explain Scrooge's descent into miserliness. The script also devotes more time to Scrooge after his transformation, especially in his interactions with the charwoman, Mrs. Dilber.

Scrooge is distinguished by a strikingly atmospheric look: stark compositions turn the film at times into an outright horror movie. The image of Scrooge sipping his soup by the fire, then jumping up in fear as he hears Marley's ghost approaching, is unforgettable, as is the austere, hooded figure of the Spirit of Christmas Yet to Come, introduced by a hand jutting into the extreme foreground on a foggy street. To design those scenes and others, producer-director Brian Desmond Hurst studied the famous illustrations done by John Leech for the first edition of Dickens's book, which had arguably been as effective as the prose in conjuring the story for those first readers. One of Hurst's most inspired touches was in casting the small role of the undertaker with Ernest Thesiger, a scene stealer who instantly brings to mind his Dr. Pretorius in *Bride of Frankenstein* (1935), another classic that mixes horror, humor, and tragedy.

Scrooge was a major hit in England in 1952, but in the United States, with the notable exception of the *New York Times*, it was dismissed by critics and failed to find an audience. Even a planned premiere at Radio City Music Hall was canceled after organizers saw the film and decided it was too bleak to be heralded as a Christmas movie. It took television airings in the 1970s and beyond for it to finally catch on in America as a classic.

Alastair Sim and Michael Hordern reprised their roles of Scrooge and Marley as voice actors for the 1971 animated short *A Christmas Carol*, which won an Academy Award. Hordern himself played Scrooge in a 1977 television movie, and *Scrooge* film editor Clive Donner later directed another version of *A Christmas Carol*, a fine 1984 release starring George C. Scott. (It was released theatrically in England and on television in America.) Even Scott, however, was no Alastair Sim, who remains the best embodiment of Dickens's enduring message that one is never too old to change, or heal, or turn one's life around.

Many of the great Christmas movies end on bursts of hope, and it may be that Dickens deserves credit as the grandfather of that tradition. While not the first author to write about Christmas, he popularized the notion that the meaning of the Christmas season can transform a soul for the better. In *Scrooge*, perhaps Tiny Tim puts this best. His father asks, "What would make Mr. Scrooge take leave of his senses suddenly?" Tiny Tim replies, "Christmas!"

BELOW LEFT: Reginald Owen as Ebenezer Scrooge and Terry Kilburn as Tiny Tim in MGM's fine, somewhat glamorized *A Christmas Carol* (1938) **BELOW RIGHT:** Michael Caine as Ebenezer Scrooge and Kermit the Frog as Bob Cratchit, along with Beaker and Bunsen Honeydew, in *The Muppet Christmas Carol* (1992), an excellent adaptation that stays true to the spirit of Dickens—and to the Muppets!

On Christmas morning, Scrooge is joyous while his charwoman (Kathleen Harrison) is dubious.

Holiday Moment

No child who has ever woken up excitedly on Christmas morning has felt anything approaching the joy of Ebenezer Scrooge on *his* Christmas morning. When Alastair Sim finds himself
alive, well, and transformed, he celebrates in a four-minute tour de force that ranks as one
of the great movie moments. He starts with fear, then moves through confusion, relief, and
excitement to infectious glee. Kathleen Harrison, as the charwoman Mrs. Dilber, is a wonderful partner to Sim in this scene, her disbelief taking a long, humorous while to dissipate.
Sim's tenderness toward her is the first compassionate act of the "new" Scrooge.

THE HOLLY AND THE IVY

British Lion, 1952 • Black and White, 83 minutes

A COUNTRY VICAR IS
OBLIVIOUS TO HIS GROWN
CHILDREN'S TROUBLES UNTIL THEY
START EMERGING DURING A
FAMILY CHRISTMAS
GATHERING.

Director
GEORGE MORE O'FERRALL

Producer
ANATOLE DE GRUNWALD

Screenplay
ANATOLE DE GRUNWALD, from the play
by WYNYARD BROWNE

Starring

RALPH RICHARDSON...............Reverend
Martin Gregory
CELIA JOHNSON ....Jenny Gregory
MARGARET LEIGHTON.......Margaret Gregory
DENHOLM ELLIOTT...........Michael Gregory
JOHN GREGSON.............David Paterson
HUGH WILLIAMS..........Richard Wyndham
MARGARET HALSTAN..............Aunt Lydia
MAUREEN DELANY.............Aunt Bridget

The Holly and the Ivy is a modest British drama that builds to a gripping conclusion. That the conclusion consists merely of two people having a frank talk in a room is actually a point in the film's favor—a tribute to excellent acting, intelligent writing, and direction that gives this stage adaptation the needed energy of a movie. The "frank" talk is key, for this is the story of a family whose dysfunction stems from unexpressed feelings and the difficulties in understanding each other's points of view. The Christmas holiday brings them together—first by placing them under the same roof, but ultimately by enabling them to *be* a family again.

Set almost entirely on Christmas Eve and Christmas Day, the story plays out in the house of a parson, Martin Gregory, in a small English town in 1948. Since his wife died earlier in the year, his grown daughter Jenny has been living at home. Martin is a good-hearted man yet so wrapped up in preparing his sermons and tending to his parishioners that he has no idea Jenny feels trapped; she wants to marry and move away

Denholm Elliott greets his aunts, played by Maureen Delany and Margaret Halstan.

but believes someone must be there to look after her father. Her brother, Michael, arrives on military leave and her sister, Margaret, arrives from London, but both also have trouble confiding in their father. All three are sure he is too conservatively religious to understand their lives and will only judge them. As Jenny says, "People just don't feel free to behave naturally when he's there." This is news to Martin, who starts to figure out what is going on and is challenged to rethink his set ways—and even his value as a parson.

The movie sprang from a 1950 play by Wynyard Browne, who based the characters on his own family. Screen rights were bought by British Lion, with the writer-producer Anatole De Grunwald heading the production. To direct, De Grunwald brought on George More O'Ferrall, a British television pioneer who had started as a theater director but made very few films. The mogul Alexander Korda held a controlling interest in British Lion, and while he had little to do with the actual making of this picture, he did arrange for an unusual production schedule: three weeks of rehearsal on the finished sets, followed by just two weeks of shooting. The plan not only saved money but helped the cast inhabit their characters completely; there's a beautiful ebb and flow to all the performances and the dialogue. As is so often the case in real life, conflicts and arguments arise gradually without becoming melodramatic.

The cast is practically a who's who of the London stage at the time, starting with Ralph Richardson. One of the great British actors, he is convincing and sympathetic as Martin Gregory, finding a quiet, doddering tone that makes his sharp outbursts all the more startling. Playing his son for the second film in a row, after *The Sound Barrier* (1952), is twenty-nine-year-old Denholm Elliott—later known for his character roles in *Trading Places* (1983) and two Indiana Jones films. The daughters are played by Celia Johnson and Margaret Leighton. Johnson is still best known to moviegoers for her Oscar-nominated turn in *Brief Encounter* (1945), but it's Leighton who steals

the picture. She has a beguiling screen presence, and her chemistry with Richardson, as a daughter and father who yearn for each other's understanding, is remarkably natural. In a way it's no surprise, for they had worked together many times on the stage, including in a famous London production of *Cyrano de Bergerac*, and Richardson was infatuated with her. They would ultimately team for four movies.

The only actors imported from the stage version of *The Holly and the Ivy* were the character actresses Margaret Halstan and Maureen Delany, who play the two aunts and provide light comic relief. One cannot be trusted with secrets, while the other criticizes and complains about everything—from the weather to the dangers of duck eggs. (What Christmas reunion doesn't have relatives like them?)

The picture opened in December 1952 in England, but not until February 1954 in America, where it was given a small art-house release. It has stood the test of time for its honest look at a family that has grown apart as it has aged, but wants to be close again. The Christmas setting, with falling snow and serenely appointed rooms, lends a stillness that seems to calm the characters and their anxieties, allowing them to finally take the chance to get things in the open and seek forgiveness.

The extraordinary kitchen scene between sisters Celia Johnson and Margaret Leighton

❊ Holiday Moment ❊

That most mundane of holiday rituals—washing the dishes after family dinner—can take on real meaning when the people doing the washing are family members reconnecting after a long time apart. In this case, one sister expresses her dilemma and asks if the other would move back home to look after their father. The response leads to the revelation of a long-held secret. Beautifully written, the scene is full of feeling without being syrupy, and Celia Johnson and Margaret Leighton capture some complex dynamics: adult siblings who are no longer a daily part of each other's lives but still feel innate compassion for one another.

WHITE CHRISTMAS

Paramount, 1954 • Color, 120 minutes

Director
MICHAEL CURTIZ

Producer
ROBERT EMMETT DOLAN

Screenplay
NORMAN KRASNA, NORMAN PANAMA,
and MELVIN FRANK

Starring

BING CROSBY . . . . Bob Wallace

DANNY KAYE . . . . Phil Davis

ROSEMARY CLOONEY . . . . Betty Haynes

VERA-ELLEN . . . . Judy Haynes

DEAN JAGGER . . . . Major General
Thomas F. Waverly

MARY WICKES . . . . Emma Allen

A PAIR OF SONG-AND-DANCE MEN
TEAM UP WITH A SISTER ACT
TO SAVE A STRUGGLING VERMONT INN
THAT'S OWNED BY THEIR BELOVED
OLD ARMY COMMANDER.

The four stars looking patriotic

O n the day in 1953 that Bing Crosby pre-recorded "White Christmas" at Paramount, Irving Berlin was pacing nervously. Crosby put an arm around him: "There's nothing we can do to hurt this song, Irving. It's already a hit!"

That was putting it mildly. In the years since Crosby first performed it in *Holiday Inn* (1942), "White Christmas" had reached number one several times and was rarely absent from the charts each December. It had sold millions of copies on the way to becoming the bestselling song in history—a record it still holds, unofficially,

since modern singles charts didn't exist until the 1950s. It had become a cultural touchstone during World War II, with Crosby traveling the globe to entertain the troops and always receiving more requests for "White Christmas" than for any other song. It had been covered by countless other artists and performed on-screen again by Crosby, in *Blue Skies* (1946). When the original master recording wore out in 1947, Crosby made a new one, the version best known today.

Because of its unceasing popularity, it was a no-brainer for Hollywood to capitalize on the song yet again. As early as 1949, *White Christmas* was in preparation at Paramount. The idea was to show off Irving Berlin tunes—old and new—and reunite the stars of *Holiday Inn*, Crosby and Fred Astaire. Berlin recycled parts of the earlier film and mixed it with elements of an unproduced musical he had written with Norman Krasna called *Stars on My Shoulders*; Krasna went on, with Norman Panama and Melvin Frank, to turn that idea into a screenplay.

Astaire declined the film, and at first so did Crosby. Within weeks, however, Crosby changed his mind, and Donald O'Connor was hired for the Astaire role. When O'Connor fell ill just before production, he in turn was replaced by Danny Kaye. To play the sisters, meanwhile, Crosby suggested singing star Rosemary Clooney, while choreographer Bob Alton proposed dance star Vera-Ellen. Michael Curtiz, who boasted *Casablanca* (1942) and *Yankee Doodle Dandy* (1942) to his credit, signed on to direct.

The result was by far the biggest hit of 1954, with the movie's nostalgia factor, Irving Berlin music, bright stars, Technicolor, and VistaVision widescreen format winning audiences over. As with *Holiday Inn*, each star received the chance to display his or her strengths. Crosby exudes effortless charm in his singing and romancing; Kaye has chances to clown, especially in "Choreography"; Clooney gives stunning renditions

of "Love, You Didn't Do Right by Me" and "Count Your Blessings Instead of Sheep," the latter an Oscar-nominated duet with Crosby; and Vera-Ellen's footwork sparkles in "Mandy," "Abraham," and "The Best Things Happen While You're Dancing."

The two women perform the fun "Sisters" number in striking blue dresses and feather fans designed by Edith Head. Clooney later joked that since she couldn't dance and Vera-Ellen couldn't sing, together they were able to pull it off. In fact, Clooney herself dubbed Vera-Ellen's singing in the number. Crosby and Kaye emit fine chemistry, too—when they spoof "Sisters," Crosby is clearly

Bing Crosby and Danny Kaye clown on the recording stage.

The four stars sing "Snow" on the train to Vermont.

struggling not to laugh as Kaye whacks him with a feather fan in a bit of improvised clowning.

But the centerpiece song is "White Christmas." It carries a different meaning here than it did in *Holiday Inn*. In that film, the song had been used more romantically than nostalgically, even though the lyrics and melody are naturally wistful. By the time of *White Christmas*, the song had become so intensely identified with nostalgia that there was really no other way to present it. Crosby sings it to soldiers in the opening World War II sequence, as he had done for real a decade earlier, and the camera pans across the men listening and yearning for home, many with their eyes closed. The set looks artificial, like a conjured memory impression, showing the point to be not realism but the nostalgia that the song and setting evoke. It's an image that resonated deeply with millions of veterans in 1954. Even now, *White Christmas* remains the holiday film best able to kindle anyone's longing for loved ones, home, or cherished moments of the past.

The grand "White Christmas" finale

Holiday Moment

During the sentimental second performance of "White Christmas," the four stars sing from a stage, clad in Santa suits, with Christmas trees next to them and falling snow behind them. The camera pulls back over the audience, which is comprised of veterans who had seen Crosby sing the song in the opening war scene. But now they aren't sitting quietly, lost in their private memories of home. They are singing joyously with Crosby and incorporating a new layer of nostalgia—for the wartime camaraderie they all experienced with each other.

WE'RE NO ANGELS

Paramount, 1955 • Color, 106 minutes

Director
MICHAEL CURTIZ

Producer
PAT DUGGAN

Screenplay
RANALD MacDOUGALL, based on a
play by ALBERT HUSSON

Starring

HUMPHREY BOGART	Joseph
ALDO RAY	Albert
PETER USTINOV	Jules
JOAN BENNETT	Amelie Ducotel
BASIL RATHBONE	Andre Trochard
LEO G. CARROLL	Felix Ducotel
JOHN BAER	Paul Trochard
GLORIA TALBOTT	Isabelle Ducotel

ON CHRISTMAS EVE, THREE
ESCAPED PRISONERS PLANNING
TO ROB A SHOPKEEPER AND
HIS FAMILY HAVE A CHANGE OF HEART
AND WIND UP HELPING
THEM INSTEAD.

ABOVE: Peter Ustinov, Aldo Ray, and Humphrey Bogart with shopkeeper Leo G. Carroll
PREVIOUS PAGE: Aldo Ray, Humphrey Bogart, and Peter Ustinov, the three "angels," survey the store.

A few months after finishing *White Christmas* (1954), director Michael Curtiz started work on *We're No Angels*, a dark comedy with a whimsical core. It was a sizable hit in the summer of 1955 but over the years has become surprisingly underrated, considering its appealing cast and consistently amusing dialogue.

The story begins on Christmas Eve, 1895, when three convicts who have escaped from prison on Devil's Island take refuge in a shop that doubles as a house. They plan to rob the place blind and kill the shopkeeper, Felix Ducotel, before hopping on a ship to France. But as they eavesdrop from the roof, they learn that Felix is not turning a profit because he extends too much credit, and that his tyrannical cousin Andre (Basil Rathbone) owns the store and controls the lives of Felix and his charming wife and daughter. Now feeling some sympathy for this family, the three men go about forging new ledgers for Felix and even selling items to customers (which generates the entertaining sight of Humphrey Bogart selling a hairbrush to a bald man). When Felix invites them to stay for Christmas dinner, they delightedly prepare everything themselves, stealing a turkey, Christmas tree, and flowers, and even cooking, setting the table, and washing the dishes. How could they possibly kill such a nice family? "After all," one of them observes, "it might spoil their Christmas." From then on, they become the family's guardian angels—as does their pet snake, Adolphe, who will deal with cousin Andre.

We're No Angels is lighthearted and absurdist from the start. The sometimes macabre dialogue and characters are buoyed by bright Technicolor photography and VistaVision clarity, and even the usual "Christmas transformation" is tongue in cheek. The three "angels" may decide not to harm the family, but the audience has never believed they would anyway—they're simply too whimsical and polite. Bogart, Aldo Ray, and Peter Ustinov make for an oddball trio. They would seem totally mismatched, but that awkwardness turns into an endearing chemistry. Bogart and Ray bring tough-guy personas that make their softheartedness and comic dialogue even funnier, while Ustinov steals his scenes by delivering witticisms with casual refinement.

Basil Rathbone (left) has arrived to inspect the ledgers, but Humphrey Bogart has other plans.

The film was adapted from a 1952 French play by Albert Husson entitled *La Cuisine des Anges* (*Angels' Cooking*). Paramount bought the screen rights shortly after the play opened in Paris and signed Julius J. Epstein, whose credits included *Casablanca* (1942), to write a treatment. The eventual screenplay was penned by Ranald MacDougall, who boasted some excellent credits himself: *Mildred Pierce* (1945) and *The Breaking Point* (1950). Meanwhile, the Husson play was adapted by Samuel and Bella Spewack for a 1953 Broadway version called *My 3 Angels*. When the film opened in 1955, some critics noticed strong similarities between that play and the movie, though Paramount insisted

Humphrey Bogart persuades a customer that a small coat fits perfectly.

it had not used the Spewacks' work. The Spewacks sued—unsuccessfully.

Paramount signed Michael Curtiz to the picture before *White Christmas* opened. No one yet knew what a box-office sensation that film would become, but Curtiz had previously struck gold with Humphrey Bogart on *Casablanca* and worked with him again on *Passage to Marseille* (1944), in which Bogart also played a Devil's Island escapee. When Curtiz joined *We're No Angels*, Bogart told Ustinov, "You gotta remember, he's got no sense of humor. So we'll just have to take things into our own hands without letting him know what we're doing." Curtiz had also directed Basil Rathbone two decades earlier in

Captain Blood (1935) and *The Adventures of Robin Hood* (1938), and Rathbone seems to be channeling those villain roles with his enjoyable nastiness here. A line like "your opinion of me has no cash value" was practically tailor-made for the man.

Joan Bennett was billed below the title for the first time since *Little Women* (1933) but was glad to be working at all. Since 1951, she had been blackballed by the industry after a notorious incident in which her husband, film producer Walter Wanger, shot her lover and agent Jennings Lang. The scandal destroyed her career, but Bogart stood by her, telling Paramount he would not do the film unless they cast her in the part. Bennett later said, "He made the stand to show what he thought of the underground movement to stamp out Joan Bennett . . . I'll never forget [his] kindness and warmth." Afterward, Bennett's career continued in fits and starts until she was cast in a long-running role on television's *Dark Shadows*.

As a Christmastime dark comedy, *We're No Angels* falls on a line that stretches from the somewhat cynical *The Man Who Came to Dinner* (1942) to *The Apartment* (1960), *Gremlins* (1984), *The Ref* (1994), and *Bad Santa* (2003). Every era, it seems, produces a classic yuletide film to satisfy our cravings for a bit of darkness amid the cheer.

Humphrey Bogart hands smelling salts to Joan Bennett as Leo G. Carroll looks on. Bogart insisted that Paramount cast Bennett, who had not had a significant role in four years.

Holiday Moment

Christmas does its "job" in the whimsical dinner sequence, transforming Bogart, Ray, and Ustinov into guardian angels. The scene is balanced by two songs. After serving dinner and unveiling the beautifully decorated (and stolen) Christmas tree, the three men sing a carol, "Three Angels," that charms the family. When the meal is over, the family retires to the living room where Joan Bennett sits at the piano and sings "Sentimental Moments," charming the men right back. That's when they decide not to cut the family's throats.

THE APARTMENT

United Artists, 1960 • Black and White, 125 minutes

WITH HOPES OF CLIMBING
THE CORPORATE LADDER,
AN OFFICE WORKER LOANS HIS
APARTMENT OUT TO HIS HIGHER-UPS
FOR THEIR EXTRAMARITAL
TRYSTS.

Director
BILLY WILDER

Producer
BILLY WILDER

Screenplay
BILLY WILDER and I. A. L. DIAMOND

Starring

JACK LEMMON . . . . C. C. Baxter
SHIRLEY MacLAINE. . . . . Fran Kubelik
FRED MacMURRAY . . . . Jeff D. Sheldrake
RAY WALSTON . . . . Joe Dobisch
JACK KRUSCHEN. . . . . Dr. Dreyfuss
DAVID LEWIS . . . . Al Kirkeby
HOPE HOLLIDAY. . . . . . Mrs. Margie MacDougall

B illy Wilder had the first inkling of what would become *The Apartment* when he saw *Brief Encounter* (1945), the classic British romance about an adulterous relationship. Struck by a scene in which the couple uses the home of a friend for their rendezvous, Wilder scrawled in his notebook afterward, "Movie about the guy who climbs into the warm bed left by two lovers." This was a potentially fascinating character who could be played for comedy or drama, he thought, but the censorship in Hollywood at the time made such a picture impossible. He decided to sit on the idea.

Thirteen years later, while directing *Some Like It Hot* (1959), Wilder realized that Jack Lemmon would be just right for the character, who had taken shape in Wilder's mind as a naïve "little nebbish." Furthermore, censorship restrictions had loosened. With his writing partner, I. A. L. Diamond, Wilder turned his idea into a story that brilliantly blended sharp comedy *and* drama. The result was far ahead of its time for its funny/tragic/sweet depiction of two people beaten down by a cynical, corrupt world—while searching for a shred of tenderness within it.

Lemmon's character, C. C. "Bud" Baxter, is an accountant at a massive New York insurance firm, a cog in the machine. He's also a bachelor with a convenient Upper West Side apartment,

ABOVE: Fred MacMurray (left) has the power over Jack Lemmon.
OPPOSITE: Shirley MacLaine and Jack Lemmon

the key to which he loans out to a rotation of philandering married executives. It's all entirely transactional: the executives need a spot for their dalliances, which are often with women from the office, and Baxter wants a promotion, even if it means occasionally being stuck outside in the freezing cold, waiting for his apartment to open up. But underneath, Baxter is tired of this dehumanizing game. He falls for a spirited elevator girl, Fran Kubelik (Shirley MacLaine), then learns that she is mired in the game herself, to a degree where tragedy is possible.

The film takes place from November 1 to January 1, with the week from Christmas to New Year's comprising most of the running time. There's certainly irony in all the heartless deceit going on at this time of year, but that's nothing compared to what Baxter and Kubelik experience on Christmas Eve and Christmas Day. At the office holiday party, hilariously staged as a bacchanal, Kubelik becomes disheartened when she starts to think— wrongly—that Baxter is simply another sleazy new executive. At the same time, Baxter recognizes Kubelik's broken compact mirror as the one he found in his apartment earlier on, and his entire conception of her changes in an instant. His devastation, in fact, comprises one of the great moments in any Billy Wilder picture, with a single shot of the mirror conveying tremendous meaning and emotion.

The rest of Christmas Eve brings further despair as Baxter drinks alone in a bar and Kubelik experiences heartbreak with another man (and that's just for starters). But Christmas Day brings the beginning of an honest connection between the two, a glimmer of hope and understanding that feels like a miracle. If the sequence were set on two other days, something would be lost—an added poignancy, a heightening of the emotions, positive

Not exactly "celebrating": Shirley MacLaine and Fred MacMurray on New Year's Eve

and negative, that are naturally magnified by the holiday season.

It's a quality that harkens back to an earlier Christmas movie, Ernst Lubitsch's *The Shop Around the Corner* (1940). Wilder revered Lubitsch, and the two films have much in common: both are set in the weeks leading to Christmas, involve workplace romance, capture the loneliness of the season, contain suicide attempts, and nonetheless drip with humanity and comic wit. *Shop* even contains a powerful moment akin to the mirror shot, in which James Stewart sees Margaret Sullavan waiting in the café and suddenly has a brand-new understanding of her—and of himself.

Director-producer-cowriter Billy Wilder on set with Shirley MacLaine

Lemmon and MacLaine were never better than here, and Fred MacMurray was a marvel as the sleazy insurance boss, Jeff D. Sheldrake. Wilder called him as a last-minute replacement for Paul Douglas, who died of a heart attack just weeks before production was set to begin. MacMurray had recently starred in *The Shaggy Dog* (1959) and was about to start shooting a new TV series, *My Three Sons*—both for family audiences. His image could not have been more different from Jeff D. Sheldrake. Wilder had to talk him into taking the role, and of course the contrast of wholesome exterior with philandering interior made him all the more effective. The same thing had happened in 1944 when Wilder cast the easygoing MacMurray as sleazy insurance agent Walter Neff in *Double Indemnity* (1944). (Had Neff survived that film, he might have spent sixteen years turning into Sheldrake!) MacMurray later told the story of visiting Disneyland sometime after *The Apartment* was released and being accosted by a woman who whacked him with her purse, complaining that this wasn't a children's movie (which she had apparently learned the hard way). "No Ma'am, it wasn't," MacMurray replied.

One of Wilder's finest achievements was never to let this film become ponderous or maudlin. The tones of sadness, sweetness, and alienation all feel equally truthful and allow the audience to find deep compassion for the characters. *The Apartment* still feels cutting-edge, and even Wilder, who didn't like to praise his own work, called it "the picture that has the fewest faults." It was honored with ten Academy Award nominations and five wins, with Wilder the first person ever to take home three Oscars for one movie: Best Picture, Director, and Original Screenplay. He shared the writing award with I. A. L. Diamond, and the master wordsmiths made their words count. When they reached the podium, Wilder said, "Thank you, I. A. L. Diamond," and Diamond replied, "Thank you, Billy Wilder."

Jack Lemmon as C. C. Baxter, drinking alone on Christmas Eve.

Holiday Moment

A costumed street Santa enters the bar on Christmas Eve for a shot of bourbon. He tries to be jovial with Baxter, who is drowning his sorrows alone and shoots St. Nick an icy stare—as if to say, "There's no place in this movie for a happy Santa Claus." He's right. When we see Santa a few minutes later, he has removed his beard and gotten drunk at the bar himself—a funny image, but one that shows even Santa to be weighed down by the harsh Manhattan of this film.

THE LION IN WINTER

Embassy Pictures, 1968 • Color, 134 minutes

IN 1183, KING HENRY II
OF ENGLAND CONVENES HIS
FAMILY FOR A CHRISTMAS COURT
TO DETERMINE THE HEIR
TO HIS THRONE.

Director
ANTHONY HARVEY

Producer
MARTIN POLL

Screenplay
JAMES GOLDMAN, based on his play

Starring

PETER O'TOOLE	Henry II
KATHARINE HEPBURN	Eleanor of Aquitaine
ANTHONY HOPKINS	Richard
JOHN CASTLE	Geoffrey
NIGEL TERRY	John
TIMOTHY DALTON	Philip II
JANE MERROW	Alais
NIGEL STOCK	William Marshal

The *Lion in Winter* is about the Christmas gathering of a dysfunctional family. It just so happens that their name is Plantagenet, their home is a castle, and when they talk about killing each other, they mean it literally. "What shall we hang?" King Henry asks, "the holly, or each other?" Dysfunction has never been so entertaining, with a powerhouse cast headed by Peter O'Toole and Katharine Hepburn that also includes some future superstars. All display terrific chemistry while clearly relishing the sharp dialogue.

James Goldman's play about King Henry II, his estranged wife Eleanor of Aquitaine, their sons, Henry's mistress, and the king of France ran for ninety-two performances on Broadway in 1966. Film producer Martin Poll optioned the property and hired Goldman to turn it into a screenplay. Peter O'Toole, Oscar-nominated for having played a younger Henry II in *Becket* (1964), happily agreed to reprise the character and even took a hand in assembling the rest of the cast: he scoured the British theater world and met with dozens of young actors, among them thirty-year-old Anthony Hopkins and twenty-one-year-old Timothy Dalton, who made their feature film debuts here. For Eleanor, O'Toole personally lobbied Katharine Hepburn, convincing her to make this her first film since

ABOVE: Katharine Hepburn as Eleanor of Aquitaine, imprisoned in Salisbury Tower. OPPOSITE: Katharine Hepburn and Peter O'Toole, loving and scheming as queen and king in front of the Christmas tree.

the death of her beloved Spencer Tracy. She also agreed with O'Toole to take a chance on director Anthony Harvey. An experienced film editor, he had directed only one feature, *Dutchman* (1966), a low-budget, black-and-white indie set entirely in a subway car.

All these moves paid off at Oscar time. Hepburn and Goldman won Academy Awards, and Harvey and O'Toole were nominated, with O'Toole becoming the second actor ever nominated twice for playing the same character. (Bing Crosby did it first.) The movie picked

The happy Plantagenet family, along with King Henry's mistress and King Philip of France. Front: Anthony Hopkins, Nigel Terry, John Castle. Rear: Jane Merrow, Peter O'Toole, Timothy Dalton, Katharine Hepburn.

the king's men. Henry has ordered her temporarily released from imprisonment at Salisbury Tower, and the moment she disembarks, their battle of wits begins: "How dear of you to let me out of jail," she says. "It's only for the holidays," he replies, one of many lines referring to Christmas and making clear that this tale will include modern dialogue. In fact, *The Lion in Winter* often feels less like historical drama and more like juicy comedy, as when Alais (Jane Merrow) tells Henry, "I can't be your mistress if I'm married to your son." "Why can't you? Johnny wouldn't mind." "I do not like your Johnny. He's got pimples and he smells of compost."

Harvey rehearsed the cast in a London theater for a week before shooting began in France, where Montmajour Abbey at Arles stood in for the castle at Chinon. More location work followed in Ireland and Wales. O'Toole and Hepburn, whose scenes comprise the heart of the film, became very close. They teased each other mercilessly, and when O'Toole showed up late to the set or wasn't exactly fresh in the morning, Hepburn would let him have it. As a result, he called her "Nags" and she called him "Pig," while underneath it all was mutual admiration and respect—exactly the dynamic between their characters onscreen.

up a third Oscar for John Barry's excellent score, as well as nominations for Best Picture and Costume Design.

Harvey said that "working with [Hepburn] is like going to Paris at the age of seventeen and finding everything is the way you thought it would be." He supplies one of Hepburn's grandest screen entrances here, placing her on a veritable throne as she is rowed to the Chinon castle grounds by ten of

There is a Christmas tree in the film, which would not have existed in twelfth-century France but adds another modern facet to the story; Christmas is an ironic counterpoint as these royal relatives tear into each other. Henry wants his youngest (and dumbest) son John to succeed him, Eleanor favors strong Richard, and meanwhile the sons scheme among themselves and against their parents. Henry is aware of all the conspiring and takes pleasure in it. "They may snap at me and plot," he says, "and that makes them the kind of sons I want. I've snapped and plotted all my life. There's no other way to be a king, alive, and fifty, all at once." The kids are just as gleeful, with Geoffrey telling his brothers early on: "Christmas! Warm and rosy time. The hot wine steams, the Yule log roars, and we're the fat that's in the fire!"

That attitude contributes to *The Lion in Winter* as an unlikely but full-fledged Christmas movie—the joy of it all. The characters find joy in their battle, the actors find joy in their dialogue, and the audience finds joy in witnessing the story come to life from such talents. Of course the film ends with laughter filling the soundtrack: it's been a bubbly ride, and there's every reason to think that come next Christmas, Henry and Eleanor will reunite, do it all over again, and love every minute of it—just like modern-day families, even the dysfunctional ones.

Holiday Moment

As they undertake the sweet Christmas ritual of placing gifts under the tree, Henry and Eleanor have their own version of "sweet" conversation: they argue over which son will receive the territory of Aquitaine and goad each other over past sexual conquests. Eleanor also gives Henry a wrapped present, which we are led to believe is his tombstone. "Eleanor," he exclaims. "You spoil me!"

A CHRISTMAS STORY

MGM, 1983 • Color, 94 minutes

Director
BOB CLARK

Producers
RENÉ DUPONT and BOB CLARK

Screenplay
JEAN SHEPHERD, LEIGH BROWN, and BOB CLARK,
based upon the novel *In God We Trust,
All Others Pay Cash* by JEAN SHEPHERD

Starring

MELINDA DILLON	Mother
DARREN McGAVIN	The Old Man
PETER BILLINGSLEY	Ralphie
SCOTT SCHWARTZ	Flick
IAN PETRELLA	Randy
TEDDE MOORE	Miss Shields
R. D. ROBB	Schwartz
ZACK WARD	Scut Farkus
YANO ANAYA	Grover Dill
JEFF GILLEN	Santa Claus
JEAN SHEPHERD	voice of adult Ralphie

AS CHRISTMAS APPROACHES
IN 1940 INDIANA, A NINE-YEAR-OLD
BOY TRIES HIS HARDEST
TO GET ONE PRESENT ABOVE
ALL ELSE: A RED RYDER 200-SHOT
RANGE MODEL AIR RIFLE.

"Christmas was on its way. Lovely, glorious, beautiful Christmas, around which the entire kid year revolved." Those lines, heard in voiceover one minute into *A Christmas Story*, perfectly set the movie's tone. They're spoken in the voice of a middle-aged man but with the timbre of a child: the voice sounds *thrilled* by the onset of Christmas. It's as if the child is trapped inside his older self's body and is doing the reminiscing.

That's the magic combination behind *A Christmas Story*: the tension between reality and nostalgia, young and old, what we hear and what we see. Scene after scene, the narrator breathlessly remembers episodes of childhood, building them up with the heightened excitement of a kid; and time after time, the visuals bring things gently back to earth, with a humor that captures the truth of it all. The movie recreates a quintessential childhood Christmas

BELOW: Christmas morning for Ralphie (Peter Billingsley, right) and his little brother Randy (Ian Petrella)
PREVIOUS PAGE: For some reason, Peter Billingsley is not happy in his pink bunny suit.

while also satirizing it, and for more than thirty years each December, American audiences have not been able to get enough.

A Christmas Story sprang from the mind of Jean Shepherd, a longtime humorist and radio personality whose on-air performances included semi-autobiographical stories based on his childhood in Indiana. He collected several of them into a book that formed the basis of the script, and it is Shepherd who narrates the picture. He is the older incarnation of Ralphie, the kid who desperately wants a Red Ryder BB gun. The trouble is, every adult who learns of his wish tells him, "You'll shoot your eye out." That deadly phrase is "not surmountable by any means known to kid-dom," Shepherd intones, but little Ralphie still tries. His quest forms the through line of the film, which otherwise is made up of vignettes depicting the charm, fun, and trauma (real and imagined) of childhood and family life.

Many of the vignettes have become beloved in American pop culture. There's the decoder ring Ralphie finally receives in the mail. He rushes to turn on his favorite radio show, *Little Orphan Annie*, to listen for a secret message, then locks himself in the bathroom for some privacy to decode it—no matter that his kid brother Randy is pounding on the door, need-

Peter Billingsley gets kicked away by Santa after a hilarious visit.

ing the toilet. (Eagle-eyed viewers can spot "1940" on the ring, the only indication of the year of this story.) There's the triple-dog-dare that leads to a schoolmate touching a frozen flagpole with his tongue. There's the bully with braces and "yellow eyes," Scut Farkas, who turns out—to no great surprise—to be a coward. And there's a brilliant sequence of Ralphie visiting an annoyed Santa Claus at the mall, heightened with surreal sound and camera angles to feel almost torturous for the kid, who is so stunned that he can't even remember what he wants for Christmas. (Jean Shepherd appears in a bit part here as a man who chastises Ralphie for cutting the line.)

In perhaps the most famous scene, a triple-dog-dare compels Flick (Scott Schwartz)
to touch a frozen flagpole with his tongue.

Then there are Ralphie's numerous daydreams about fending off bad guys with his air rifle, getting an A+++++ on a school essay, and going blind as revenge against Mom because she made him wash his mouth out with soap after he dropped an F-bomb in front of "the old man" (his father).

The episodes involving the entire family are warmly real and involve just the kinds of tiny moments that someone would remember from childhood, as when the old man receives his "indescribably beautiful" leg lamp in the mail. This causes a look of alarm on Mom's face as she realizes it will be prominently placed in the living room—and entices Ralphie in a classic bit of business to slide his hand up the "leg." Later on, when Ralphie realizes that Mom is not going to tell the old man about Ralphie's fight with the bully, he exchanges a smile with her that is among the most heartwarming memories. "From then on," Shepherd narrates, "things were different between me and my mother."

A Christmas Story was a dream project for director Bob Clark, whose films up to that point included the Christmas slasher film *Black Christmas* (1974) and the raunchy comedy *Porky's* (1981). He had wanted to make a movie from Shepherd's work since first hearing him on the radio twelve years earlier. MGM supplied a small budget of $4.4 million, and Clark even kicked in an extra $150,000 of his own money.

To cast Ralphie, Clark first saw eleven-year-old Peter Billingsley, an experienced child actor with television shows and numerous commercials under his belt, but the director went on to consider hundreds of other kids before recognizing Billingsley as the perfect choice. For the parents, Clark cast two-time

Melinda Dillon sets up the leg lamp (prized by her husband, dreaded by her) as Peter Billingsley watches.

RIGHT: Over-bundled Ian Petrella can barely move as he walks to school with Peter Billingsley, R. D. Robb, and Scott Schwartz.

BELOW: Peter Billingsley is feeling superconfident after handing in his essay on what he wants for Christmas.

Oscar nominee Melinda Dillon and the seasoned Darren McGavin, whose varied career dated back to 1945. The film was shot in Cleveland and Toronto, and Clark later said "it was joyful" to work with Billingsley, Ian Petrella (who plays Randy), and all the other kids, who display remarkable chemistry on-screen.

The movie opened to generally positive reviews at Thanksgiving but was not given many screens. Critic Roger Ebert predicted that "either nobody will go to see it, or millions of people will go to see it," and in a way he was right on both counts. Despite making a profitable, though still modest, $19 million at the box office, *A Christmas Story* was gone from theaters by Christmas, elbowed out by bigger films. In the years that followed, however, audiences fell in love with it on home video and then cable television, with the Turner networks TNT and TBS airing it in

Ralphie and his family mesmerized by the Christmas parade. From left: Peter Billingsley, Ian Petrella, Darren McGavin, Melinda Dillon

twenty-four-hour marathons every Christmas. It's now a seasonal juggernaut as indispensable and beloved as *It's a Wonderful Life* (1946) and *Miracle on 34th Street* (1947).

Holiday Moment

Ralphie and his little brother Randy open two presents on Christmas morning to find socks inside, and the look they exchange is priceless because it's so relatable. But "priceless" doesn't begin to describe Ralphie's reaction to what he unwraps next: a pink bunny suit from Aunt Clara. Probably every kid has an Aunt Clara—as well as a mother who would make the kid try that bunny suit on right away.

GREMLINS

Warner Bros., 1984 • Color, 106 minutes

A CUDDLY, EXOTIC PET SPAWNS HUNDREDS OF MISCHIEVOUS LITTLE MONSTERS THAT DESCEND UPON A TOWN AT CHRISTMASTIME.

Director
JOE DANTE

Producer
MICHAEL FINNELL

Screenplay
CHRIS COLUMBUS

Starring

ZACH GALLIGAN . . . . Billy
PHOEBE CATES . . . . Kate
HOYT AXTON . . . . Rand Peltzer
POLLY HOLLIDAY . . . . Mrs. Deagle
FRANCES LEE McCAIN . . . . Lynn Peltzer
JUDGE REINHOLD . . . . Gerald
DICK MILLER . . . . Mr. Futterman
GLYNN TURMAN . . . . Roy Hanson
KEYE LUKE . . . . Grandfather
SCOTT BRADY . . . . Sheriff Frank
COREY FELDMAN . . . . Pete
JONATHAN BANKS . . . . Deputy Brent
EDWARD ANDREWS . . . . Mr. Corben
HARRY CAREY, JR. . . . . Mr. Anderson

irector Joe Dante's horror comedy straddles the line between unsettling and hilarious, sending up Christmas, and movies—and yes, Christmas movies—without falling into sentiment. It begins when traveling salesman Rand Peltzer (Hoyt Axton), browsing in an almost otherworldly Chinese gift shop, comes upon a strange but adorable little animal. It's called a Mogwai, says the store owner (Keye Luke), and it's not for sale. But Rand finagles a purchase from the owner's grandson, who tells him there are three simple rules that must be followed with this creature: keep him out of the light, keep him away from water, and never—never!—feed him after midnight.

Rules are made to be broken, of course, and the consequences in *Gremlins* are mayhem, death, and destruction—all coated with gleeful humor. Rand gives the Mogwai to his son, Billy (Zach Galligan); Billy names him Gizmo; and

BELOW: Gremlins singing Christmas carols with pint-sized sheet music.
OPPOSITE: Gentle Gizmo hides from the mean gremlins. Gizmo was voiced by Howie Mandel.

Stripe, the gremlin leader, has a bead on Billy.

the rule-breaking results in hundreds of mischievous, murderous offspring called gremlins. These little ghouls cause trouble all over town and wholeheartedly enjoy it, which is why it's so easy to laugh with *Gremlins*. The movie is frightening at times but never really becomes pure horror because the gremlins are just too much fun. They sing Christmas carols; they take over a bar to drink, smoke, and play cards while ransacking the place; they wear Santa hats, feast on Christmas cookies, and attempt to sing "Jingle Bells"; they take over a movie theater and watch *Snow White and the Seven Dwarfs* (1937), singing along with the film and throwing popcorn. They even operate the movie projectors, semi-successfully. These scenes look like a crazy alternate universe of *The Muppet Show*, because the gremlins are all portrayed by meticulously crafted puppets.

Gremlins inhabits a world of classic movies, with frequent references to sci-fi/horror classics of Dante's youth and to *It's a Wonderful Life* (1946). The town here is called Kingston Falls, à la Bedford Falls, and it has many of the same types of establishments lining the main street. Billy works in a bank and is even filmed in a version of James Stewart's run through the snowy streets. There's also a "Mr. Potter" character named Mrs. Deagle, a mean old woman

Keye Luke, whose screen career started in 1934, as the Chinese "Grandfather" who knows the secrets of the gremlins

whose stair-lift is a nod to Potter's wheelchair and figures uproariously in her screen exit.

The term "gremlin" became popular during World War II, used by air crews to refer to fictional creatures responsible for engine malfunctions. Roald Dahl wrote a 1943 children's book about gremlins, and Walt Disney nearly used Dahl's ideas for an animated film. This movie, however, began in the New York loft of screenwriter Chris Columbus. He heard mice scampering across the floor as he tried to fall asleep and started imagining them as monsters

Hoyt Axton with a Mogwai Christmas present for son Billy (Zach Galligan),
as Frances Lee McCain looks on.

in the dark; he turned that thought into a straight horror script in which the gremlins killed people horribly and were not funny or cute. Intended as a writing sample, the script found its way to Steven Spielberg, who found it so original that he purchased it to executive-produce for his new company, Amblin Entertainment. (*Gremlins* was the first film to carry the Amblin logo, which appears at the end of the credits.)

Spielberg suggested cutting way down on the horror and keeping Gizmo as a lovable creature throughout, rather than having him transform into a nasty gremlin as originally devised. When Joe Dante came on as director, he injected black humor and made the first half of the story much warmer in tone. That way, he said, "even the smallest amount of violence became a little bit more intense."

The filming process was grueling. Each gremlin was controlled by at least three tech-nicians using wires and cables. For scenes with many gremlins in the frame, the crew built a raised platform to serve as the set, with a large mass of technicians, wires, and monitors underneath. The actors did a fine job reacting credibly to the puppets, but the bar scene just about wrecked Phoebe Cates. For three days, crew members threw things at her because that's what the gremlins do. "I hated everybody after that scene," she said. "I didn't want to see another gremlin for a week."

Gremlins was a box office hit in the summer of 1984, but not without controversy. Its violence angered parents who thought they were taking their young kids to see a sweet puppet comedy. *Indiana Jones and the Temple of Doom* (1984), released two weeks earlier and also rated PG, caused similar reactions, and the result was a new ratings category—PG-13—which was inaugu-rated later that summer with *Red Dawn* (1984).

Holiday Moment

At first, the Peltzer family kitchen is a lovely holiday setting, as Billy's mother (Frances Lee McCain) bakes Christmas cookies. Minutes later, it's a battlefield, as she fends off gremlins with the help of all sorts of kitchen instruments. Like the movie as a whole, it's all a bit horrible as well as funny.

DIE HARD

Twentieth Century-Fox, 1988 • Color, 132 minutes

A NEW YORK COP BATTLES TERRORISTS WHO HAVE SEIZED A LOS ANGELES SKYSCRAPER AND TAKEN HOSTAGES.

Director
JOHN McTIERNAN

Producers
LAWRENCE GORDON and JOEL SILVER

Screenplay
JEB STUART and STEVEN E. DE SOUZA, based on a novel by RODERICK THORP

Starring

BRUCE WILLIS . . . . John McClane
ALAN RICKMAN . . . . Hans Gruber
ALEXANDER GODUNOV . . . . Karl
BONNIE BEDELIA . . . . . . Holly Gennaro McClane
REGINALD VELJOHNSON . . . . Sergeant Al Powell
WILLIAM ATHERTON . . . . Thornburg
PAUL GLEASON . . . . Dwayne T. Robinson
HART BOCHNER . . . . Ellis
JAMES SHIGETA . . . . Takagi
ANDREAS WISNIEWSKI . . . . Tony
CLARENCE GILYARD, JR. . . . . Theo
DE'VOREAUX WHITE . . . . Argyle

ABOVE: Reginald VelJohnson and Paul Gleason as Los Angeles gets a "white Christmas," thanks to falling office paper
OPPOSITE: Bruce Willis as John McClane, a cop doing his job on Christmas Eve

Is *Die Hard* the story of terrorists who take over a building on Christmas Eve, only to have their plans disrupted by a pesky cop named John McClane? Or is it the story of a cop named John McClane who tries to reconcile with his estranged wife on Christmas Eve, only to have his plans disrupted by pesky terrorists?

Ultimately it's both, but the second perspective, which is the one that leads the audience into the film, is the start of a common Christmas-movie plot: a dysfunctional family reuniting over the holidays. One of the pleasures of *Die Hard* is that once the action starts, it doesn't let go of the Christmas movie elements but rather transforms them into action movie variations, all with a cheerful humor that itself represents the season. For instance, Santa Claus appears in the form of a dead terrorist wearing a Santa hat (a long way from Edmund Gwenn!). The same terrorist is wearing a

A plot device keeps Bruce Willis in bare feet throughout—boosting the humor, vulnerability, and heroism of his character.

sweater on which McClane has scrawled the immortal words, "Now I have a machine gun, Ho-Ho-Ho"—the ultimate ugly Christmas sweater. The usual Christmas-movie "house" is here the entire Nakatomi Plaza, basement to roof, and instead of dwelling in the nice rooms containing holiday decorations, McClane spends his time scampering through elevator shafts, air vents, and partially built floors—a perfect home for an action hero. There's even a white Christmas in L.A., courtesy of falling office paper.

There are smaller touches of the season, too, such as playful dialogue referring to Christmas ("It's the time of miracles," says Hans); a variety of Christmas music worked into the soundtrack, including sleigh bell effects at key moments; and two character names that were changed from the source novel. The book's "Stephanie" became the film's "Holly," a much more Christmassy name, and the novel's Anton Gruber became Hans Gruber—which sounds suspiciously like Franz Gruber, the Austrian composer of "Silent Night." But the main holiday theme remains the reconciliation story between John and Holly McClane. John recognizes his faults and finds some Christmas redemption in the matter while he is exhausted, bleeding, and holding a gun—and he's not even talking to Holly, but rather to Al Powell, the LAPD officer, over a walkie-talkie. In an action movie like this, there's no time for any other way.

Die Hard was adapted from the novel *Nothing Lasts Forever* by Roderick Thorp, who got his idea after seeing *The Towering Inferno* (1974) and dreaming about a man chased through a tall building by bad guys with guns. (He wrote it as a sequel to *The Detective*, which had been turned into a 1968 film with Frank Sinatra.) The original screenplay for *Die Hard* was so serious that director John McTiernan insisted on making it "more entertaining and less horrifying." He had the German terrorists altered to be stylish and upscale, and he changed their mission from one of politics to an elaborate heist. That allowed the movie to take on a lighthearted tone, even as McTiernan packed it with gun battles, explosions, and death-defying stunts, all suspenseful and expertly paced. *Die Hard* is violent but not cruel or unpleasant. In its own way it exudes a sense of joy that allows it to connect better to Christmas than other action movies set over the holiday season, including *Die Hard 2*, which is not really a Christmas movie.

Bruce Willis certainly brought humor with him, though his casting was controversial

Hanging by a hose: Bruce Willis outside Nakatomi Plaza in an expertly crafted action scene

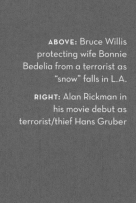

ABOVE: Bruce Willis protecting wife Bonnie Bedelia from a terrorist as "snow" falls in L.A.

RIGHT: Alan Rickman in his movie debut as terrorist/thief Hans Gruber

CHRISTMAS IN THE MOVIES

for just that reason. Known at the time for the TV show *Moonlighting*, he was thought to be far too light and comedic to make a convincing action hero. In the end, his more normal-looking physique—as opposed to action superstars Sylvester Stallone or Arnold Schwarzenegger—made him appealingly vulnerable, and his humorous, blue-collar grit set an appealing tone that has helped *Die Hard* endure. When Hans (played with humor and menace by Alan Rickman in his screen debut) taunts McClane about wanting to be like John Wayne, McClane replies that he actually always preferred Roy Rogers—"I really liked those sequined shirts"—and he tells Hans to call him "Roy." Perhaps McClane had seen the real Roy's own Christmas film, *Trail of Robin Hood*.

Holiday Moment

Is there anything more satisfying on Christmas than watching a loved one open the perfect present? Maybe watching it twice over. First up in *Die Hard* is Hans Gruber. Thanks to his own hard work of planning the robbery, he gives himself the greatest present possible: finally breaking into the vault with $640 million in bearer bonds within. The movie lets the audience share Hans's triumph by blasting Beethoven's "Ode to Joy" and lovingly panning over the bonds and other treasures. "Merry Christmas," says a henchman.

McClane gives himself the perfect present, too—his own trusty Beretta 92F pistol, which he even "giftwraps" for himself with holiday packing tape. When he "unwraps" it at a pivotal moment, the audience gets the gift of watching him put it to sensational use and live up to his cowboy likeness. *Yippee ki-yay, Christmas movie!*

NATIONAL LAMPOON'S
CHRISTMAS VACATION

Warner Bros., 1989 • Color, 97 minutes

CLARK GRISWOLD'S PLANS FOR A PERFECT FAMILY CHRISTMAS ARE CHALLENGED BY ONE COMIC MISHAP AFTER ANOTHER.

Director
JEREMIAH CHECHIK

Producers
JOHN HUGHES and TOM JACOBSON

Screenplay
JOHN HUGHES

Starring

CHEVY CHASE	Clark Griswold
BEVERLY D'ANGELO	Ellen
RANDY QUAID	Cousin Eddie Johnson
MIRIAM FLYNN	Cousin Catherine Johnson
WILLIAM HICKEY	Lewis
MAE QUESTEL	Bethany
DIANE LADD	Nora
JOHN RANDOLPH	Clark, Sr.
E. G. MARSHALL	Art
DORIS ROBERTS	Francis
JULIETTE LEWIS	Audrey
JOHNNY GALECKI	Rusty
NICHOLAS GUEST	Todd Chester
JULIA LOUIS-DREYFUS	Margo Chester
BRIAN DOYLE-MURRAY	Frank Shirley

ABOVE: Chevy Chase and E. G. Marshall take cover from a squirrel on the loose. OPPOSITE: The Griswold family: Clark and Ellen (Chevy Chase and Beverly D'Angelo), with their kids Audrey and Rusty (future stars Juliette Lewis and Johnny Galecki)

All Clark Griswold wants is "a fun, old-fashioned family Christmas." He'll take his family into the woods to cut down a Christmas tree; decorate the outside of the house with lights; enjoy the pleasant company of relatives; and host a delicious turkey dinner. He'll also use the nice, fat bonus he expects from his boss to cover the cost of a new swimming pool. That would all be lovely, wouldn't it? There's just one problem: this is a *Vacation* movie, which means that even getting to the woods will be a death-defying ordeal.

National Lampoon's Christmas Vacation is a comedy of mayhem resulting from good intentions, a tradition that dates back to the silent-era days of Laurel and Hardy and Buster Keaton. Murphy's Law applies—everything that can

ABOVE: A tad overcooked? Clark (Chevy Chase) slices what's left of the Christmas turkey. Far side of table, from left: Beverly D'Angelo, E. G. Marshall, and Doris Roberts

RIGHT: Merry Christmas, Clark! Cousin Eddie (Randy Quaid) has proudly snatched Clark's boss, Frank Shirley (Brian Doyle-Murray), and adorned him with "a big ribbon"— per Clark's wishes, which were not meant to be taken literally.

go wrong will go wrong. Clark (Chevy Chase) staples the lights to the roof but only after some hair-raising adventures on the ladder, and getting those lights to work will create just the first of many electrical disasters. The relatives arrive, but one can forget the word "pleasant." The work bonus is not exactly what Clark had in mind, and as for the turkey, let's just say it's the crunchiest in movie history.

There's something to laugh at every few seconds, but the gags are not all throwaway. Some build slowly over the course of the story to grand payoffs, such as Cousin Eddie (Randy Quaid) draining his mobile home's septic tank into the sewer. Others build within seconds from the simplest actions, like climbing a ladder or riding a sled coated with grease. Then there are the enjoyable quirks, such as drinking from moose mugs, which is a nod to the first *Vacation* film, and violent set pieces treated as pure comedy—an electrocuted cat, a fall from a roof, the kidnapping of Clark's boss. When a SWAT team arrives to the strains of Gene Autry's "Here Comes Santa Claus," the tone is just right. Clark's wife, Ellen (Beverly D'Angelo), sums up everything well: "It's Christmas, and we're all in misery."

Actually, Clark is too much the eternal optimist to feel miserable. "Christmas is about

The tree isn't too big for the living room, just "a little full," Clark signals.

resolving differences and seeing through the petty problems of family life," he says, a line that draws a laugh but also shows why Clark is so endearing. His hopeful enthusiasm, in fact, provides much of the movie's heart and keeps it from being just a succession of gags. Chevy Chase was already a fixture in the role, having played Clark Griswold in the first two films of the series, *National Lampoon's Vacation* (1983) and *National Lampoon's European Vacation* (1985), which were based on stories in the *National Lampoon* parody magazine. All three were written by John Hughes, one of the era's comedy geniuses. As producer, Hughes first

Aunt Bethany's cat chewing the Christmas tree
lights—yet another recipe for disaster

the voices of Betty Boop and Olive Oyl in
the 1930s. Here she's a hoot as the batty Aunt
Bethany, who wraps up her cat as a Christmas
present and recites the pledge of allegiance at
the dinner table when asked to say grace. Also
on hand: Juliette Lewis and Johnny Galecki,
both of whom would later soar to stardom, and
a pre-*Seinfeld* Julia Louis-Dreyfus as one of the
yuppies living next door.

Chechik later remembered the gags as
requiring many hours or even days to shoot.
For the riotous scene in which "Snots" the
dog chases a squirrel through the house,
both animals were trained for months; then,
on the day of filming, the squirrel suddenly
died. "They don't live that long," the trainer
told Chechik, who now had no choice but to
use an untrained squirrel. "It was just total
chaos," Chechik recalled.

There have been two further *Vacation* sequels,
but *Christmas Vacation* is the highest-earning and
perhaps best entry to date. It's certainly still the
most widely seen. With the superb comic timing
of Chevy Chase, an overriding sense of festive
cheer, and even a groovy holiday soundtrack that
includes Ray Charles, Bing Crosby, and Mavis
Staples, it's no wonder that watching the Gris-
wolds try to navigate Christmas has become an
annual tradition.

offered the directing reins to Chris Columbus, but Columbus clashed with Chevy Chase
and soon withdrew. Hughes gave him a top-
notch consolation prize—the chance to direct
Home Alone (1990)—and replaced him with
Jeremiah Chechik, a fashion photographer
and director of commercials making his first
feature film.

Chechik had not only a great script but
an outstanding cast, from comedy mainstays
Chase, D'Angelo, and Quaid, who was born
for the part of dimwitted Cousin Eddie, to
veterans Diane Ladd, E. G. Marshall, and
eighty-year-old Mae Questel, who had created

The calm before the storm as the grandparents arrive: John Randolph, Doris Roberts, E. G. Marshall, and Diane Ladd

❄ *Holiday Moment* ❄

Alone in the house, Clark gets trapped in the attic in his pajamas. First he suffers through a series of physical calamities that show the house as essentially one giant weapon—an idea John Hughes would take to even more inventive lengths in his script for *Home Alone*. But then Clark finds a 16mm projector and a box of old home movies, and he decides to pass the time by watching a film of his childhood Christmas. For a sweet minute or two, he forgets his troubles and is even brought to tears, thanks to the magic combination of movies, nostalgia, and the season.

HOME ALONE

Twentieth Century-Fox, 1990 • Color, 103 minutes

WHEN HE'S ACCIDENTALLY LEFT BEHIND BY HIS VACATION-BOUND FAMILY, AN EIGHT-YEAR-OLD DEFENDS HIS HOUSE AGAINST DIMWITTED BURGLARS.

Director
CHRIS COLUMBUS

Producer
JOHN HUGHES

Screenplay
JOHN HUGHES

Starring

MACAULAY CULKIN	Kevin McCallister
JOE PESCI	Harry Lime
DANIEL STERN	Marv
JOHN HEARD	Peter McCallister
ROBERTS BLOSSOM	Old Man Marley
CATHERINE O'HARA	Kate McCallister
ANGELA GOETHALS	Linnie
DEVIN RATRAY	Buzz
GERRY BAMMAN	Uncle Frank
HILLARY WOLF	Megan
JOHN CANDY	Gus Polinski

The second Christmas movie in a row from writer-producer John Hughes hit the sweet spot. *National Lampoon's Christmas Vacation* (1989) had been a surprise hit, but *Home Alone* became a global phenomenon. It has aged extremely well: its humor hasn't dated, its look is still warm and inviting, and Macaulay Culkin remains as lovable as ever. But the movie's secret weapon is really fantasy—of the wish-fulfillment kind.

When young Kevin McCallister discovers his family is gone, he thinks it's because he wished them away in a moment of irritation the night before, and his first reaction is one of delight in his power. He runs around the house, gorges on junk food and television, and snoops through his mean older brother's room, feeling like the luckiest kid in the world. Later, he heroically battles two burglars with ingenious booby-traps and becomes, essentially, the smartest kid in the world. All the while, *Home Alone* offers reminders that Kevin is still a normal little boy underneath, as he thinks with charmingly kid-like logic and inevitably starts to miss his family. He cuts down a small tree to decorate for Christmas, sets up stockings over the fireplace, and even ventures out to ask a costumed Santa, quite sincerely, to please bring his family home. Christmas, he learns, isn't really Christmas without them.

ABOVE: Buzz devours the last slice of cheese pizza, much to Kevin's annoyance. **OPPOSITE:** "Do you guys give up, or you thirsty for more?"

John Hughes said he got the idea for *Home Alone* right before a family trip to Paris. He was going over a list of things not to forget when he wondered what would happen if he "forgot" his youngest child. He quickly wrote a few pages of notes; when he returned ten days later, he knocked out a screenplay in a little over a week, imagining Macaulay Culkin in the lead. (Hughes had just directed him in *Uncle Buck* [1989].) At this time, Hughes was on a creative and professional roll, writing and directing a movie a year while also writing and producing many others—most of them hits. He offered *Home Alone* to young director Chris Columbus, who was originally to have directed *National Lampoon's Christmas Vacation*, with the promise of creative autonomy. Columbus went about auditioning two hundred kids before finally meeting with Macaulay Culkin and realizing he was, in fact, ideal. He even cast Macaulay's little brother Kieran in his screen debut as a bedwetting cousin.

To play the comical burglars known as the "Wet Bandits," Columbus went with the inspired combination of Joe Pesci and Daniel Stern, who inject shades of Laurel and Hardy into their scenes. Pesci took his part after

Robert De Niro and Jon Lovitz each turned it down, and the result was an extraordinary year for the actor: when *Home Alone* opened, *Goodfellas* (1990) was already in release, with a menacing Pesci performance that would win him an Oscar.

Home Alone was set to be produced by Warner Bros. until shortly before production, when a dispute over a slight budget increase prompted Warners to drop the film—a decision that stands as one of the great missteps in Hollywood history. Fox immediately picked the film up, approved a final budget of $18.2 million, and watched it become the

Daniel Stern and Joe Pesci, the "Wet Bandits"

ABOVE: While singing in the bathroom to the Drifters' 1954 cover of "White Christmas," Macaulay Culkin slaps on some aftershave, leading to this iconic moment. The script called for the hands to go to the face, but Culkin improvised holding them there for the entire scream that followed.

LEFT: Macaulay Culkin trims the tree but Joe Pesci has other plans.

The McCallister kitchen. Production designer John Muto applied a red-and-green motif to all the interiors, even the props and wallpaper, to lend a seasonal feel.

highest-grossing live action comedy of all time (a record it still holds), grossing $285 million domestically and $470 million worldwide. In fairness, however, no one could have foreseen quite that level of success.

Columbus shot the movie in the Chicago area, with the McCallister house located in the North Shore suburb of Winnetka, where it still attracts fans. The final battle between Kevin and the burglars, involving irons to the head, falls on icy steps, and hard smashes into walls, required top-notch stuntmen. Columbus later told an interviewer that he wasn't laughing as they worked: "I would just pray that the guys

were alive." Daniel Stern felt that way himself when he performed a shot with a tarantula on his face. He dubbed his scream later because a real scream would have scared the tarantula.

In the finished film, the stunts come off as cartoonishly hilarious, not least because they are the result of a child's ideas for booby-traps. *Home Alone* incorporates a childlike perspective throughout, down to its camera angles. Cinematographer Julio Macat explained that the angles were wider, the camera was lower, and the lighting was brighter because "kids see everything in an amplified way." The movie also keeps a steady Christmas feel with red and green worked into the production design and the costumes, as well as a festive soundtrack of holiday tunes and a touching score. John Williams, a late addition when the original composer had to bow out, would receive both of the film's Oscar nominations, for Score and Song.

The yuletide tone culminates in a heartwarming Christmas Day finale involving Culkin and Catherine O'Hara, who has spent most of the story fighting to get back home to him. She has even traveled all night in the back of a van with John Candy and his polka band because, after all, what would Christmas be without her son?

Holiday Moment

Before his final battle with the Wet Bandits, Kevin takes a breather by visiting a church to listen to a choir. While there, he has a talk with Old Man Marley, the "scary" neighbor played by Roberts Blossom, whom all the kids think is a serial killer called the South Bend Shovel Slayer. Kevin learns he's actually a nice old guy with an estranged son, and they each offer the other some advice on family. Columbus called this his favorite scene and said not one word of Hughes's dialogue was altered.

Mother and son reunited: Catherine O'Hara and Macaulay Culkin

THE NIGHTMARE BEFORE CHRISTMAS

Buena Vista, 1993 • Color, 76 minutes

JACK SKELLINGTON, THE "PUMPKIN KING" OF HALLOWEEN TOWN, KIDNAPS SANTA AND TAKES OVER CHRISTMAS.

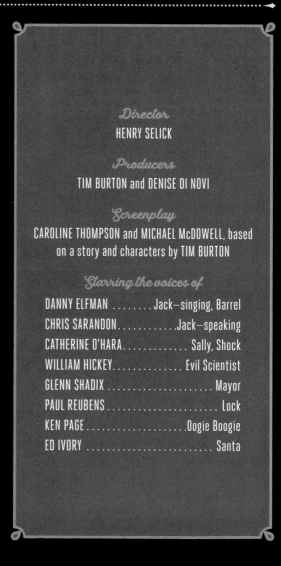

Director
HENRY SELICK

Producers
TIM BURTON and DENISE DI NOVI

Screenplay
CAROLINE THOMPSON and MICHAEL McDOWELL, based on a story and characters by TIM BURTON

Starring the voices of
DANNY ELFMAN . . . . Jack—singing, Barrel
CHRIS SARANDON . . . . Jack—speaking
CATHERINE O'HARA . . . . Sally, Shock
WILLIAM HICKEY . . . . Evil Scientist
GLENN SHADIX . . . . Mayor
PAUL REUBENS . . . . Lock
KEN PAGE . . . . Oogie Boogie
ED IVORY . . . . Santa

"What's this? There's color everywhere!" sings Jack in Christmas Town.

Imagine if Halloween and Christmas had their own towns, each with residents, colors, sounds, and even weather in complete contrast to the other. Imagine if a dapper skeleton from Halloween Town found his way to Christmas Town and was amazed and enchanted by all he saw there. And imagine if he then decided it would be fun to kidnap Santa and organize Christmas himself this year. What could possibly go wrong?

The Nightmare Before Christmas is a wonderfully inventive musical fable told in the medium of stop-motion animation. The age-old technique involves photographing puppets or other objects one frame at a time, slightly manipulating the figures between shots to create the illusion of movement with a unique, "handmade" feel. It has mostly been used for short films, or special effects in longer ones, while remaining a rare choice for an entire feature. But *The Nightmare*

RIGHT: Jack thought the serpent would be an adorable present.

BELOW: The mayor of Halloween Town with two of his illustrious citizens.

Before Christmas began in the fertile mind of Tim Burton, who had long wanted to combine his two favorite holidays into one story and pay tribute to the stop-motion classics he had loved as a child—from the television special *Rudolph the Red-Nosed Reindeer* (1964) to the work of innovators Ray Harryhausen and George Pal.

In his downtime as a Disney animator in 1980, he doodled skeleton figures and eventually wrote his story as an illustrated poem, thinking it could be made as a television special itself. Disney found it too bizarre and macabre a concept at the time, but by 1990, after Burton had become a commercially successful filmmaker, the studio was interested and gave a green light. With Burton committed to directing *Batman Returns* (1992), which incidentally is also set over Christmas, he decided to produce *The Nightmare Before Christmas* and hand the directing reins to Henry Selick, a friend from his Disney animation days who had since done much stop-motion work. Selick and Burton saw eye to eye on the tone of the movie, drawing inspiration from Dr. Seuss, illustrators Edward Gorey and Charles Addams, and even the classic Robert Mitchum thriller *The Night of the Hunter* (1955), which has a fairy-tale quality and a Christmas element.

Filming began in 1991 at a San Francisco production facility. For two years, a team of

Jack asks rag doll Sally to make his "Sandy Claws" outfit; she thinks his plan is a bit misguided.

artists overseen by Selick used twenty animation stages to shoot the film frame by frame. With twenty-four frames per second and a story length of about seventy-one minutes (without credits), that came to over one hundred thousand frames. Many of the seventy-four puppet characters had hundreds of versions of eyes, eyelashes, and other parts available. Jack Skellington alone had four hundred puppet heads that could be clicked into place as needed, each with the tiniest variation of facial expression.

But none of Jack's heads had eyeballs. Like many Burton protagonists—and the classic movie monsters that inspired them—Jack Skellington is a misunderstood outsider. "He looks scary, but really isn't," Burton said, and the lack

Santa is unaware his big night will not go as planned.

of eyeballs conveys that notion inventively. It also happens to violate what Burton called "the first rule of animation, to give your characters expressive eyes," and it was a sticking point with Disney until Burton prevailed. Jack's heart and soul come to life through his other features and his voice—especially his singing voice, supplied by Danny Elfman and overflowing with whimsy and longing. Elfman was Burton's frequent composer and wrote the movie's ten songs before the script was even finished.

All this artistry culminated in a memorable film that skirts between comedy and mild fright with an overriding tone of cheer. When Jack experiences Christmas for the first time, he is transformed (as happens so often in Christmas movies) from a melancholy fellow into a joyous one, singing, "In my bones I feel the warmth that's coming from inside." He also is charmed that kids would be "throwing snowballs instead of throwing heads."

The Nightmare Before Christmas was a modest hit in 1993 and in the years since has grown into a true classic. Converted to 3-D in 2006, it still enjoys a limited re-release in certain cities each Halloween season, giving rise to a debate over whether it is a "Halloween movie" or a "Christmas movie." Humbug—it's both!

Holiday Moment

The image of Santa delivering presents takes on a wickedly funny variation here. Dressed as Santa, Jack soars over Christmas Town in a sleigh pulled by skeletal reindeer, dropping off ghoulish presents that not only horrify kids and their parents, but in some cases attack them. Jack believes he's doing something delightful and can't understand why anyone in Christmas Town would be trying to shoot him from the sky.

Sally, beautifully voiced by Catherine O'Hara (the mother in *Home Alone*), yearns for Jack's love.

LITTLE WOMEN

Columbia, 1994 • Color, 115 minutes

**THE MARCH SISTERS GROW
FROM ADOLESCENCE
INTO ADULTHOOD IN CONCORD,
MASSACHUSETTS, DURING AND
AFTER THE CIVIL WAR.**

Director
GILLIAN ARMSTRONG

Producer
DENISE DI NOVI

Screenplay
ROBIN SWICORD, based on the novel
by LOUISA MAY ALCOTT

Starring

WINONA RYDER	Jo March
GABRIEL BYRNE	Friedrich Bhaer
TRINI ALVARADO	Meg March
SAMANTHA MATHIS	Older Amy March
KIRSTEN DUNST	Younger Amy March
CLAIRE DANES	Beth March
CHRISTIAN BALE	Laurie
ERIC STOLTZ	John Brooke
JOHN NEVILLE	Mr. Laurence
MARY WICKES	Aunt March
SUSAN SARANDON	Mrs. March

Louisa May Alcott's *Little Women* has long been a beloved American novel, but in the early 1990s that was not a good enough reason for Columbia Pictures to approve a new screen version. It was only when studio executive Amy Pascal pitched it to her bosses as a Christmas movie that they finally saw a marketing angle and gave a green light—smart thinking all around, for the result was a box-office hit and the finest *Little Women* picture to date. It even picked up three Oscar nominations, for Best Actress (Winona Ryder), Costume Design, and Score.

It wasn't a stretch to boost the yuletide atmosphere. After all, Alcott did write Christmas sequences into the novel, and this is the tale of a family, a story in which everything feels most right when the March sisters and their mother are together. Headstrong Jo, steady Meg, shy Beth, and vain Amy grow up in 1860s New England through episodes ranging from harmonious to vindictive, but

BELOW: Winona Ryder as Jo **OPPOSITE:** Marmee with her girls on Christmas Eve. From left: Jo (Winona Ryder), Meg (Trini Alvarado), Amy (Kirsten Dunst), Marmee (Susan Sarandon), and Beth (Claire Danes)

ABOVE: The March sisters bringing their Christmas breakfast to the less fortunate: Claire Danes, Trini Alvarado, Winona Ryder, Kirsten Dunst

RIGHT: Mary Wickes, so memorable in *The Man Who Came to Dinner* (1942) and *White Christmas* (1954), made her last screen appearance as Aunt March. Katharine Hepburn was offered this role but declined.

their fundamental closeness outweighs all else. There's a truth to the characters that makes them timeless—even Jo's vicious anger after she discovers Amy has burned her manuscript feels honest in this film, not melodramatic.

Alcott modeled the characters on her own family, with Jo, the tomboyish, aspiring writer, based on Alcott herself. She composed the book in two volumes, and its instant success led her to write two sequels. She never cared much for *Little Women*, however, referring to it as "moral pap for the young" and noting that she only wrote it because her publisher was pressuring her for a "girls' story." Nonetheless, the novel has never been out of print and has been adapted to the stage and screen many times.

Amy Pascal and screenwriter Robin Swicord had wanted to collaborate on a new film of *Little Women* for over a decade before Pascal's rise through the Hollywood ranks finally led to this chance. Pascal (who was named after Amy March) brought on Denise Di Novi to produce, who in turn suggested Winona Ryder to play Jo; Di Novi and Ryder had long been attracted to the story themselves and discussed it while making *Heathers* in 1988. To direct, Di Novi and Pascal hired the fine Australian filmmaker Gillian Armstrong, whose sensitivity to wom-

Christian Bale as Laurie

en's stories had been obvious since her acclaimed first feature, *My Brilliant Career* (1979).

The Christmas season is a grounding force in this movie. It sets the tone before any characters are shown—even before the opening credits are done—with images of a wreath being placed on a door and a Christmas tree being pulled on a sled through the snow. (These shots and a few others were filmed in the well-preserved town of Deerfield, Massachusetts.) Thomas Newman's orchestral score evokes the snug warmth of the season, and Winona Ryder's voiceover conjures nostalgia, family, and coziness: "My sisters and I remember that winter as the coldest of our childhood." This efficient setup takes all of a

TOP: In RKO's lauded 1933 version, Marmee (Spring Byington) is surrounded by her "little women": Beth (Jean Parker), Amy (Joan Bennett), Jo (Katharine Hepburn), and Meg (Frances Dee).

BOTTOM: MGM's 1949 remake was in glossy Technicolor: Beth (Margaret O'Brien), Amy (Elizabeth Taylor), Meg (Janet Leigh), and Jo (June Allyson). Not pictured: Mary Astor as Marmee or Leon Ames as Mr. March, who had also played husband and wife in *Meet Me in St. Louis* (1944).

few seconds before the March sisters are seen clamoring to the door to welcome home their "Marmee" (Susan Sarandon) on Christmas Eve. Later on, there will be another happy homecoming during a second Christmas sequence, but *Little Women* is actually filled with reunion scenes, and they're all treated as joyously as the ones on Christmas, thereby cementing the idea of family togetherness as meaningful to this story. When Jo asks at one low point, "Will we never all be together again?" it sounds like the worst thing in the world that could happen to these characters.

The feel of the season remains when Christmas is over, thanks to more snowy scenes and a pervading sense of nostalgia—even as Swicord's script works in progressive themes of women's rights and their roles in society, borrowed from the real-life Alcott family's beliefs in transcendentalism. There are men in the story, mainly two suitors played by Christian Bale and Gabriel Byrne as well as a father, but the women—and the idea of family—remain the focus. (The father spends much of the story off-screen, even after he returns from service as an army chaplain in the Civil War.)

Little Women was perfectly cast. Ryder had just appeared in the very modern *Reality Bites* (1994) but was nonetheless at home in period films, having starred in *The Age of Innocence* (1993); Claire Danes was making a huge splash in her TV series *My So-Called Life*, which was still airing when this film opened on December 21, 1994; and Kirsten Dunst, all of twelve, was rising fast in the industry herself. The showy part of Aunt March found a fine character actress in eighty-three-year-old Mary Wickes, who had started her career with one Christmas film, *The Man Who Came to Dinner* (1942), and made her final appearance with this one.

Holiday Moment

After the ailing Beth comes downstairs for the movie's second Christmas celebration, she is presented with a piano and sits down to play "Deck the Halls." All the gathered family and friends join in for some spirited singing in a scene that radiates joy and warmth. As Aunt March says afterward, in a line that sounds ad-libbed by Mary Wickes, "That was good!"

ELF

New Line Cinema, 2003 • Color, 97 minutes

A HUMAN RAISED BY ELVES LEAVES THE NORTH POLE TO SEARCH FOR HIS FATHER IN NEW YORK.

Director
JON FAVREAU

Producers
JON BERG, TODD KOMARNICKI, and SHAUNA ROBERTSON

Screenplay
DAVID BERENBAUM

Starring

WILL FERRELL	Buddy
JAMES CAAN	Walter
ZOOEY DESCHANEL	Jovie
MARY STEENBURGEN	Emily
DANIEL TAY	Michael
EDWARD ASNER	Santa
BOB NEWHART	Papa Elf
FAIZON LOVE	Gimbels manager
PETER DINKLAGE	Miles Finch
AMY SEDARIS	Deb

When *Elf* opened in late 2003, director Jon Favreau said his fondest hope was that it would become an annual Christmas staple. Before the film even finished its theatrical run, it seemed clear that his hope would come true: *Elf* was a massive success, a sweet, funny, smart fantasy for all ages.

Filmmaking is a collaborative art, but it's fair to say that Favreau worked hard to get a very personal vision of the story on the screen. The script by David Berenbaum had been floating around Hollywood since 1993, originally written with Jim Carrey in mind. It had been optioned a few times before landing in front of Favreau, who had directed and written one small film, *Made* (2001), and written another, *Swingers* (1996). (He also acted in both.) At first he didn't care for *Elf,* finding the script too dark, but then he saw how it could be transformed into something lighter, with wider appeal. He spent a year rewriting it, injecting the unabashed innocence into the Buddy character that would prove so winning to audiences. The result still had some edge but mostly embraced a fairy-tale quality and childlike enthusiasm. As Favreau put it, "I wanted to keep it a PG movie, not a PG-13 movie that made fun of Christmas."

He also decided to avoid computer-generated imagery in favor of old-fashioned, practical effects such as models and matte paintings. Computer effects, he thought, might soon look dated, and he was eager to pay tribute to the classic Christmas movies and television specials he had loved growing up. That's why the North Pole character of Leon the Snowman, voiced by jazz singer Leon Redbone, was created with stop-motion animation—as a nod to the 1960s TV specials *Frosty the Snowman* and *Rudolph the Red-Nosed Reindeer,* the latter of which also inspired the design of the elf costumes.

BELOW: Just another day in New York: Will Ferrell stopping traffic OPPOSITE: "Santa's coming?! I know him!!" Will Ferrell as Buddy and Faizon Love as the manager of the Gimbels "North Pole" department

For scenes at Santa's Workshop, in which Buddy towers over the elves, furniture, and appliances, Favreau worked with his crew to use forced perspective. With this age-old technique, two sets were created for single shots: one very small set in the foreground, with small-scale props and furniture, and a second very large set in the background, with oversized items. When lined up meticulously and lit just right, they gave the illusion of a single set. Actors on one set, however, could look much bigger than actors on the other.

Edward Asner as a down-to-earth Santa

Elf started production in December 2002, a little over a year after the 9/11 attacks. As a native New Yorker, Favreau was passionate about doing his part to prevent New York from being redefined in people's minds. Creating a heartwarming Christmas fantasy that showed the city in beautiful holiday mode was a way of reclaiming it. "I wanted to make something escapist and hopeful for kids from New York," he said. While most of the film was shot in Vancouver (including all interiors), Favreau did as much location work as possible in Manhattan, including a scene at the Rockefeller Center ice rink and part of the Central Park sequence. On the last day of production, Favreau and a small camera crew walked around the city filming Will Ferrell in elf attire as he improvised interactions on the streets.

Originally Favreau wanted the store in the film to be Macy's, as a nod to the quintessential New York Christmas movie, *Miracle on 34th Street* (1947). The company had one condition: the department store Santa in *Elf* could not be revealed as a fake Santa. Macy's felt such a scene would ruin their Christmas image established by the earlier picture. Favreau wouldn't alter the scene but he kept the *Miracle* connection by using the name Gimbels, which had been Macy's competitor in *Miracle* as well as in real life—until

Will Ferrell in school with young elves at the North Pole

1987, when it went out of business. Favreau was wise to keep the "fake Santa" scene as scripted, for it's one of the best in the picture. Will Ferrell's sheer excitement over what he thinks will be a visit by Santa Claus is indelible, as is the realization that this Santa (played by Artie Lange) is actually a fraud. "You sit on a throne of lies!" Ferrell exclaims, before ripping off Santa's beard to the delight of assembled kids.

Ferrell had just left the cast of *Saturday Night Live*, and Favreau had to insist to his producers that he was the right choice for a family-friendly comedy. Zooey Deschanel's career had been rising fast since her turn in *Almost Famous* (2000), and when Favreau discovered that she was also a singer, he incorporated singing into the script: Deschanel performs a memorable rendition of "Baby, It's Cold Outside" with Ferrell, and singing even becomes a vital plot device at the film's climax. Favreau made a third inspired casting choice in James Caan, who plays Buddy's father. The oddness of tough-guy

ABOVE: Will Ferrell in Santa's Workshop. Peter Billingsley, who starred as Ralphie in *A Christmas Story*, stands at left wearing glasses, as an elf named Ming Ming. Billingsley has also been a producer on two other Jon Favreau films: *Zathura* (2005) and *Iron Man* (2008).

RIGHT: Will Ferrell and Zooey Deschanel in Gimbels.

Amy Sedaris and James Caan don't know what to make of Will Ferrell.

Caan even being in a movie where he interacts with a grown man in an elf costume makes his character's unease all the more amusing.

Elf is a pure Christmas movie, completely embracing the season with the eagerness of a child—or at least a man-child—and instilling that eagerness into the audience. When Santa shows up again toward the end, landing his sled in Central Park, likely everyone watching will feel like a kid, which is a lovely gift from Favreau. He gives himself a small part, incidentally, as a doctor, and voices a few creatures at the North Pole, including the narwhal who says, "Bye, Buddy. Hope you find your dad."

Holiday Moment

New York at Christmastime is enchanting to begin with, but when combined with the image of Santa and his reindeer soaring over Manhattan, accompanied by John Debney's rousing score, it becomes magical.

LOVE ACTUALLY

Universal, 2003 • Color, 135 minutes

LOVE IS EXPERIENCED ACROSS NINE INTERLACED STORIES DURING THE WEEKS LEADING UP TO CHRISTMAS IN LONDON.

Director
RICHARD CURTIS

Producers
DUNCAN KENWORTHY, TIM BEVAN, and ERIC FELLNER

Screenplay
RICHARD CURTIS

Starring

ALAN RICKMAN.....................Harry
BILL NIGHY ....Billy Mack
COLIN FIRTH.......................Jamie
EMMA THOMPSON..................Karen
HUGH GRANT............The Prime Minister
LAURA LINNEY......................Sarah
LIAM NEESON ....Daniel
MARTINE McCUTCHEON ....Natalie
ANDREW LINCOLN....................Mark
CHIWETEL EJIOFOR..................Peter
GREGOR FISHER ....Joe
HEIKE MAKATSCH ....Mia
KEIRA KNIGHTLEY...................Juliet
KRIS MARSHALL ....Colin Frissell
LUCIA MONIZ.....................Aurelia
MARTIN FREEMAN ....John
RODRIGO SANTORO....................Karl
THOMAS SANGSTER....................Sam
ROWAN ATKINSON ....Rufus, Jewelry
                                 Salesman
BILLY BOB THORNTON......The U.S. President

ABOVE: Prime Minister Hugh Grant, on a high after telling off the U.S. president, dances to the Pointer Sisters' "Jump" inside 10 Downing Street. OPPOSITE: Liam Neeson helps stepson Thomas Sangster wade through his romantic "agony."

*L*ove *Actually* opened on November 7, 2003, the same day as *Elf.* Both have become annual holiday viewing for countless fans, though at the time they found quite different audiences. *Elf,* a comic fantasy for all ages, was a huge hit in the United States but only a modest performer abroad; *Love Actually,* a romantic comedy primarily for grown-ups, earned much more abroad than it did in the United States. (In the end, *Love Actually* grossed $247 million worldwide, to *Elf*'s $220 million.)

Love Actually falls in the tradition of multiple-story, multiple-star vehicles dating back to *Grand Hotel* (1932), cutting among nine essentially self-contained tales. All are love stories of some sort—romantic, platonic, parental, sibling—and they cover a spectrum from poignant to comedic, realistic to absurd. There's a hilarious story of an aging pop star and former drug addict trying for a comeback with a new Christmas version of an old hit (the real-life 1967 Troggs single "Love Is All Around," redone as "Christmas Is

Married Alan Rickman is tempted by vixen Heike Makatsch.

All Around"); the rocker constantly berates his manager but deep down would be lost without their friendship. There's a writer who falls for his Portuguese housekeeper in the south of France, despite neither of them understanding a word of the other's language. There's a best man at a wedding who's secretly in love with the bride, an office employee who pines for her handsome coworker, a Prime Minister who can't stop thinking about a member of the Downing Street staff, and more. In some cases, love conquers all; in others, it does not.

Writer-director Richard Curtis originally planned to make two movies, one centering on the Prime Minister character (played by Hugh Grant) and the other on the writer (Colin Firth). As he worked the ideas out in his mind, he realized they were too similar to previous films he had written, such as *Four Weddings and a Funeral* (1994) and *Notting Hill* (1999). It would be better, Curtis decided, if he could combine them into one script with several other plot strands so that the movie overall would be about love in many forms. For inspiration, he turned to the films of Robert Altman, whose *Nashville* (1975) was a famous example of the multistory approach. Then, while taking daily walks on a beach in Bali, where he was recuperating from a back ailment, Curtis pondered his own past romances and those of his friends to come up with seven more story lines. When he sat down to write, his goal was to find "nine good beginnings and nine good endings with no dull stuff in between."

It was only when he got to about page thirty that Curtis had the idea of setting the film in the weeks leading to Christmas. The big day itself serves as a stage for the characters to finally open up or discover the truth of their situations. Love, in effect, ends up being the ultimate Christmas gift. There's a bit of "Scrooge"-like transformation, too, in the pop

ABOVE: Bill Nighy's buoyant turn as "the bad grand-dad of rock and roll" made him an international star.

LOWER RIGHT: Keira Knightley had just appeared in *Bend It Like Beckham* (2002) and *Pirates of the Caribbean: The Curse of the Black Pearl* (2003) and was soaring to stardom.

LOWER LEFT: Emma Thompson as Alan Rickman's wife, with William Wadham as their son

The romance between Prime Minister Hugh Grant and secretary Martine McCutcheon comes unexpectedly out in the open.

star played by Bill Nighy, who for most of the movie is very unsentimental about the holiday. But perhaps the cleverest Christmas-movie element comes at the end, when characters from most of the stories enjoy mini-reunions, one after the other, at the airport arrival hall. The effect is of a single, massive, joyful family reunion. It doesn't matter that the scene actually takes place a month after Christmas, or even that most of these characters are completely unaware of the other stories happening around them—after being interwoven for two hours of screen time, they have come to feel like one big family for the audience.

Curtis made a splashy directing debut with *Love Actually*. He gathered a large cast that combined major British stars (and Americans Laura Linney and Billy Bob Thornton) with lesser-known actors who have since become stars themselves, including Chiwetel Ejiofor, Andrew Lincoln, Martin Freeman, and January Jones. The picture shot for thirteen weeks in the fall of

2002 in London, the south of France, and Heathrow Airport, where a camera crew captured the opening and closing documentary-like footage. These montages of real reunions sprang from an experience Curtis had at an airport years earlier, watching people explode into hugs and affection as they found their loved ones. "Everyone in a crowd has a special story," he observed. "A real story, a love story."

Love Actually has been critiqued for its implausible story lines, and even Richard Curtis admitted to some tonal inconsistencies, telling *Variety*, "I'm not sure all the stories are from the same universe." Dissecting all the stories for rationality, however, is beside the point. Of course it's not "rational" that the Prime Minister would dance around 10 Downing Street to the Pointer Sisters; or that an ordinary English bloke (Kris Marshall) would fly to Wisconsin in search of romance, and sure enough find three stunning, interested babes in a bar within minutes of arriving in Milwaukee; or that a twelve-year-old boy (Thomas Sangster) would run through the airport, chased by security, to say good-bye to the girl of his dreams. After all, this is the same kid who tells his stepfather (Liam Neeson) that nothing "could be worse than the total agony of being in love." The kid is right. Who's to say what is "rational" when it comes to matters of the heart—or to sugar-coated Christmas movies that celebrate the season with romance and humor?

Holiday Moment

As Otis Redding's cover of "White Christmas" plays on the soundtrack, Colin Firth arrives at his sister's house on Christmas Eve, arms full of presents. "Uncle Jamie! Uncle Jamie!" the kids exclaim as the family comes to the door. Suddenly, Firth realizes this isn't right; he needs to get to the Portuguese love of his life (Lucia Moniz), somewhere, somehow, right away. He turns around to depart, leaving everyone stunned—except for those little kids, who now hilariously declare, "I hate Uncle Jamie!" It's as if Firth stumbled into the wrong Christmas movie, about relatives returning home for the holidays, before coming to his senses and remembering that he's actually in his *own*, quite different, Christmas film.

BIBLIOGRAPHY

In addition to the sources listed, information came from production files, clippings, studio publicity notes, and trade paper reviews held at the Academy of Motion Picture Arts and Sciences' Margaret Herrick Library.

BOOKS

Astaire, Fred. *Steps in Time*. New York: Harper & Brothers, 1959.

Atkins, Irene Kahn. *Henry Koster: A Directors Guild of America Oral History*. Metuchen, NJ: Scarecrow Press, 1987.

Barbour, Alan G. *Humphrey Bogart*. New York: Pyramid, 1973.

Basinger, Jeanine. *The "It's a Wonderful Life" Book*. New York: Knopf, 1986.

———. *Shirley Temple*. New York: Pyramid, 1975.

———. *The Star Machine*. New York: Knopf, 2007.

Bennett, Joan, and Lois Kibbee. *The Bennett Playbill*. New York: Holt, Rinehart and Winston, 1970.

Berg, A. Scott. *Goldwyn: A Biography*. New York: Knopf, 1989.

———. *Kate Remembered*. New York: Putnam, 2003.

Behlmer, Rudy. *Memo from David O. Selznick*. New York: Viking, 1972.

Black, Shirley Temple. *Child Star*. New York: McGraw-Hill, 1988.

Bowman, Manoah. *Natalie Wood: Reflections on a Legendary Life*. Philadelphia: Running Press, 2016.

Carey Jr., Harry. *Company of Heroes: My Life as an Actor in the John Ford Stock Company*. Metuchen, NJ: Scarecrow Press, 1994.

Chierichetti, David. *Mitchell Leisen: Hollywood Director*. 2nd ed. Los Angeles: Photoventures Press, 1995.

Clooney, Rosemary, with Joan Barthel. *Girl Singer: An Autobiography*. New York: Doubleday, 1999.

Cox, Stephen. *It's a Wonderful Life: A Memory Book*. Nashville: Cumberland House, 2003.

Crowe, Cameron. *Conversations with Wilder*. New York: Knopf, 1999.

Curtis, James. *Between Flops: A Biography of Preston Sturges*. New York: Harcourt, Brace, Jovanovich, 1982.

Dick, Bernard. *Hollywood Madonna: Loretta Young*. Jackson: University Press of Mississippi, 2011.

Eliot, Marc. *Cary Grant: A Biography*. New York: Harmony Books, 2004.

Emery, Robert J. *The Directors: Take Two*. New York: Media Entertainment, 2000.

Everson, William K. *The Hollywood Western*. Secaucus, NJ: Carol Pub. Group, 1992.

Eyman, Scott. *John Wayne: The Life and Legend*. New York: Simon & Schuster, 2014.

Finstad, Suzanne. *Natasha: The Biography of Natalie Wood*. New York: Harmony Books, 2001.

Fraga, Kristian, ed. *Tim Burton: Interviews*. Jackson: University Press of Mississippi, 2005.

Furia, Philip. *Irving Berlin: A Life in Song*. New York: Schirmer Books, 1998.

Green, Stanley, and Burt Goldblatt. *Starring Fred Astaire*. New York: Dodd, Mead & Company, 1973.

Harvey, James. *Romantic Comedy in Hollywood: From Lubitsch to Sturges*. New York: Knopf, 1987.

Hoberman, J. "The 'Gremlins' Franchise: Standing Spielberg on His Head." In *Joe Dante* by Nil Baskar and Gabe Klinger. Vienna: Synema, 2013.

Honeycutt, Kirk. *John Hughes: A Life in Film*. New York: Race Point, 2015.

Koenig, David. *Danny Kaye: King of Jesters*. Irvine, CA: Bonaventure Press, 2012.

Leigh, Janet. *There Really Was a Hollywood*. Garden City, NY: Doubleday, 1984.

Levinson, Peter J. *Puttin' on the Ritz: Fred Astaire and the Fine Art of Panache*. New York: St. Martin's Press, 2009.

Lichtenfeld, Eric. *Action Speaks Louder: Violence, Spectacle, and the American Action Movie*. Westport, CT: Praeger, 2004.

Maland, Charles J. *Frank Capra*. Boston: Twayne Publishers, 1980.

Malone, Aubrey. *Maureen O'Hara: The Biography*. Lexington: University Press of Kentucky, 2013.

Marill, Alvin. *Katharine Hepburn*. New York: Pyramid, 1973.

Marshall, J. D. *Blueprint on Babylon*. Tempe: Phoenix House, 1978.

Martin, Hugh. *Hugh Martin: The Boy Next Door*. Encinitas, CA: Trolley Press, 2010.

McBride, Joseph. *Frank Capra: The Catastrophe of Success*. New York: Simon & Schuster, 1992.

McGilligan, Patrick. *Ginger Rogers*. New York: Pyramid, 1975.

Miller, John. *Peter Ustinov: The Gift of Laughter*. London: Orion Books, 2003.

———. *Ralph Richardson: The Authorized Biography*. London: Sidgwick & Jackson, 1995.

O'Hara, Maureen, with John Nicoletti. *'Tis Herself: An Autobiography*. New York: Simon & Schuster, 2004.

Osterholm, J. Roger. *Bing Crosby: A Bio-Bibliography*. Westport, CT: Greenwood Press, 1994.

Peary, Danny. *Cult Movies 3*. New York: Simon & Schuster, 1988.

Pettigrew, Terence. *British Film Character Actors*. Totowa, NJ: Barnes & Noble Books, 1982.

Phillips, Robert W. *Roy Rogers*. Jefferson, NC: McFarland, 1995.

Quirk, Lawrence J. *Margaret Sullavan: Child of Fate*. New York: St. Martin's Press, 1986.

Rode, Alan K. *Michael Curtiz: A Life in Film*. Lexington: University Press of Kentucky, 2017.

Rosen, Jody. *White Christmas: The Story of an American Song*. New York: Scribner, 2002.

Salisbury, Mark, ed. *Burton on Burton*. London: Faber and Faber, 2000.

Schary, Dore. *Heyday: An Autobiography*. Boston: Little, Brown and Company, 1979.

Server, Lee. *Robert Mitchum: Baby, I Don't Care*. New York: St. Martin's Press, 2001.

Sikov, Ed. *Dark Victory: The Life of Bette Davis*. New York: Henry Holt, 2007.

———. *On Sunset Boulevard: The Life and Times of Billy Wilder*. New York: Hyperion, 1998.

Simpson, Mark. *Alastair Sim: The Star of Scrooge and The Belles of St. Trinian's*. Stroud, England: The History Press, 2008.

Soren, David. *Vera-Ellen: The Magic and the Mystery*. Baltimore: Luminary Press, 2003.

Taravella, Steve. *Mary Wickes: I Know I've Seen That Face Before*. Jackson: University Press of Mississippi, 2013.

Thompson, Dave. *Winona Ryder*. Dallas: Taylor Publishing, 1996.

Thomson, David. *Showman: The Life of David O. Selznick*. New York: Knopf, 1992.

Tranberg, Charles. *Fred MacMurray: A Biography*. Albany, GA: BearManor Media, 2007.

Wallis, Hal, and Charles Higham. *Starmaker*. New York: Macmillan, 1980.

Weinberg, Herman G. *The Lubitsch Touch: A Critical Study*. New York: Dover Publications, 1977.

Wilder, Alec. *American Popular Song: The Great Innovators, 1900–1950*. New York: Oxford University Press, 1972.

Willoughby, Bob. *The Star Makers: On Set with Hollywood's Greatest Directors*. London: Merrell, 2003.

PERIODICALS

Abele, Robert. "'Elf' for the Holidays." *Los Angeles Times*, November 2, 2003.

Avins, Mimi. "Ghoul World." *Premiere*, November 1993.

Blaisdell, George. "Seeing Some Films." *American Cinematographer*, April 1940.

Denby, David. "Always Making Wisecracks." *Premiere*, November 1990.

De Turenne, Veronique. "Love Actually." *Variety*, January 4, 2004.

Dreyfuss, Ben. "Why 'Love Actually' Matters." *Mother Jones*, December 9, 2013.

Felperin, Leslie. "Animated Dreams." *Sight and Sound*, December 1994.

Friedwald, Will. "The Song That Changed Christmas Forever." *The Wall Street Journal*, October 4, 2016.

Goldstein, Patrick. "The Big Picture." *Los Angeles Times*, September 10, 2003.

Guadagnino, Kate. "Why 'Little Women' Is Still the Best Christmas Movie." *Vogue*, December 24, 2015.

Horowitz, Josh. "The Mind of the Modern Filmmaker." *New York* magazine, November 10, 2003.

"Hugh Martin's 'Hidden Treasures' Explored." Interview on *Fresh Air* program transcribed into online article. National Public Radio, December 22, 2011.

Hughes, James. "Holy Cow, 'Home Alone' Is 25!" *Chicago* magazine, December 2015.

"Jack Skirball Out as GN-Educat'l V.P." *Variety*, July 12, 1939.

Kashner, Sam. "How 'A Christmas Story' Went from Low-Budget Fluke to an American Tradition." *Vanity Fair*, November 30, 2016.

LeDonne, Rob. "Xmas or Bust: The Untold Story of 'National Lampoon's Christmas Vacation.'" *Rolling Stone*, December 22, 2014.

MacFarquhar, Larissa. "Sweet 'N' Jo." *Premiere*, January 1995.

McCarthy, Todd. "Deep Focus: Christmas Presents of All Kinds." *Variety*, November 21, 2003.

———. "McTiernan Keeps Highrise Action Earthy." *Variety*, July 25, 1998.

Minter, George. "Why I Chose Sim." *Picturegoer*, August 25, 1951.

Mitchell, Elvis. "Q&A with Joe Dante." *Los Angeles Reader*, June 15, 1984.

Stern, Marlow. "'Love Actually's' 10th Anniversary." *The Daily Beast*, November 7, 2013.

Warren, Elaine. "'Gremlins' Features Live Creatures, Too." *Los Angeles Herald-Examiner*, June 5, 1984.

ONLINE DATABASES

afi.com/members/catalog

ibdb.com

imdb.com

mediahistoryproject.org

nyu.edu/projects/wke/index.php

tcm.com

Fred MacMurray and Barbara Stanwyck break out the popcorn in *Remember the Night*.

INDEX

James Stewart and Donna Reed fall in love in *It's a Wonderful Life*.

ACKNOWLEDGMENTS

I am grateful to many friends and colleagues for their help in the writing of this book. I thank them for their generous time, insight, and enthusiasm, and especially for being willing to think and talk about Christmas movies at an "off" time of year. They all easily earned their wings, as Henry Travers would say.

The finest wings at Macy's (or Gimbels, if Macy's doesn't have them) must go to Cindy De La Hoz, who brought me this idea and is more than just my editor for the second book running—she is a patient, supportive friend.

My dear pal and fellow movie fanatic Mark Cantor went above and beyond to offer much helpful feedback, and his expertise as a music historian was invaluable to me.

Other friends who kindly read drafts along the way and gave thoughtful comments include Eric Lichtenfeld, who probably knows more about *Die Hard* than even those who made it, Owen Renfroe, Nancy Valen, Farrah Boutia, Veronica Chandler, and Tamsen Wolff, who loves *Little Women*.

To Jeanine Basinger—film scholar and keeper of the Frank Capra collection at the Wesleyan University Cinema Archives—I offer my deepest thanks for thirty years of teaching and friendship.

Thanks also to Sam Wasson, Steven C. Smith, David Arnold, Alice Arnold, Jonathan Arnold, Gael Arnold, Susan Landesmann, Scott Eyman, Don McGlynn, Patricia Ward Kelly, Ron Borst, Margaret Borst, Alan K. Rode, Avis Wrentmore, Jeff Mantor at Larry Edmunds Bookshop, Frank Tarzi at Kino Lorber, Ned Comstock at the USC Cinematic Arts Library, Eddie Brandt's Saturday Matinee, and the entire staff of the Margaret Herrick Library at the Academy of Motion Picture Arts and Sciences, an invaluable resource without which this book would not have been possible.

At TCM, thanks are in order to longtime friends and colleagues who directly and indirectly helped with this project: John Malahy, Heather Margolis, Scott McGee, Genevieve McGillicuddy, Pola Changnon, Jennifer Dorian, Ben Mankiewicz, Charles Tabesh, Sean Cameron, Quatoyiah Murry, Shannon Clute, and Kristen Welch.

Finally, I offer my sincere gratitude to Aaron Spiegeland at Parham Santana, book designer Jason Kayser, publicist Seta Zink, Running Press publisher Kristin Kiser, and the late TCM host Robert Osborne, a continued source of inspiration for his superlative movie expertise coupled with the kindest of hearts.